Where Women Create
Book of Inspiration

Where Women Create
Book of Inspiration

In the Studio & Behind the Scenes with Extraordinary Women

Jo Packham • Jenny Doh

LARK BOOKS
A Division of Sterling Publishing Co., Inc.
New York / London

Library of Congress Cataloging-in-Publication Data

Packham, Jo.
Where women create : book of inspiration : in the studio & behind the scenes
with extraordinary women / Jo Packham & Jenny Doh. -- 1st ed.
p. cm.
Includes index.
ISBN 978-1-60059-564-6 (hc-plc with jacket : alk. paper)
1. Artists' studios. 2. Women artists. 3. Women designers. I. Doh, Jenny. II.
Title.
N8520.P34 2010
704'.042--dc22

2009034456

10 9 8 7 6 5 4 3 2

WRITER & EDITOR
Jenny Doh

COPY EDITOR
Christen Olivarez

DESIGNER
Raquel Joya

Published by Lark Books, A Division of
Sterling Publishing Co., Inc.
387 Park Avenue South, New York, NY 10016

Text © 2010, Jo Packham, Jenny Doh
Photography © 2010, *Where Women Create*

Distributed in Canada by Sterling Publishing,
c/o Canadian Manda Group, 165 Dufferin Street
Toronto, Ontario, Canada M6K 3H6

Distributed in the United Kingdom by GMC Distribution Services,
Castle Place, 166 High Street, Lewes, East Sussex, England BN7 1XU

Distributed in Australia by Capricorn Link (Australia) Pty Ltd.,
P.O. Box 704, Windsor, NSW 2756 Australia

If you have questions or comments about this book, please contact:
Lark Books
67 Broadway
Asheville, NC 28801
828-253-0467

Manufactured in China

ISBN 13: 978-1-60059-564-6

For information about custom editions, special sales, premium and corporate
purchases, please contact Sterling Special Sales Department at 800-805-5489
or *specialsales@sterlingpub.com*.

Dedications

My mother, my daughter, my grandchildren … it is you who make me want to be a better person. For you I work harder, reach higher, and travel farther than I ever would for myself. I love each of you from the bottom of my heart and the very depth of my soul … for all the same and yet for so many different reasons.

— Jo Packham

I dedicate this book to Kellene Giloff, whose creativity, tenacity, and sincerity have deeply influenced and inspired me over the years. And also to the loving memory of my grandmother, Kwang Eun Kim, a creative genius who taught me that with imagination and fortitude, you can create almost anything out of practically nothing.

— Jenny Doh

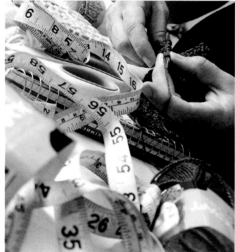

Where Women Create
Book of Inspiration

In the Studio & Behind the Scenes with Extraordinary Women

Jo Packham • Jenny Doh

CONTENTS

Introduction

For many, the idea of creating something from nothing is an impossible task. Or at least it's a task that requires some degree of magic. After all, how can nothing become something? During my childhood in Seoul, Korea, I grew up in a household where the women in my family performed magic every day … as humble ingredients became delicious pots of soup to feed all who came to the dinner table, and old sweaters became unraveled and knitted back up into garments for the littlest ones in the family. Growing up, I saw magic happen.

In 2005, Jo Packham also made magic happen by creating a book that would become the authority in showcasing the studio spaces of creative women — *Where Women Create: Inspiring Work Spaces of Extraordinary Women* (Sterling, 2005). It was a book that started with nothing but a vision to offer breathtaking photographs alongside compelling narratives of some of the most artistic and passionate women of our time.

In 2008, Jo partnered with Stampington & Company to launch *Where Women Create* magazine for a most enthusiastic readership — a quarterly periodical that would continue the traditions of the book to feature the unique studio spaces of artistic women.

For the book that you hold in your hands today, *Where Women Create: Book of Inspiration* (Sterling, 2010), it has been my honor and privilege to work with Jo to take the chronicles of *Where Women Create* to the next level. In addition to *our* own stories, we have convened 21 distinguished artists who offer exclusive tours of their stunning studios, along with special behind-the-scenes insight into their unique sources for inspiration.

Through the process of interviewing all of the featured women to write their profiles, I became fascinated to learn about the many different ways in which artists become motivated to create. Some are inspired by music, others by color. One is inspired by pop culture, another by natural light, and still another by shadows.

And for some, inspiration is found in both the joys and sorrows of life, as they create art that helps them cope with the bad and celebrate the good.

The individuals profiled in this book are extremely diverse and tremendously talented. Knitters, painters, jewelry artisans, photographers, mixed-media artists, quilters, writers, doll makers, and fashion designers are who you will get to know.

Alongside each of their narratives, you will encounter gorgeous photographs of the artists' spaces, as well as images that illustrate their sources for inspiration. You'll also enjoy samples of some of their most prized creations.

In addition, this most creative cohort provides valuable organizational tips and ideas, along with fun exercises to enhance creativity. Enchanting memories from their childhood, favorite color palettes, and suggestions on how to combat ruts are also included throughout the book.

Despite the diversity of their work, there is a common denominator that unifies all of the incredible women, which is that they are all able to create something from nothing. Every day, as they wrestle with the challenge of juggling multi-tasks of home life and studio life, or the pressure of fulfilling huge orders or managing tight deadlines, the artists all know how to find a way to make it happen.

From the bottom of my heart, and on behalf of the entire team that has worked so hard to put this book together, I thank you for joining us on this journey as we discover through the pages of *Where Women Create: Book of Inspiration* the exciting wonders of creativity, inspiration, and magic.

Jenny Doh

Danita

Danita is a mixed-media artist whose colorful art dolls, paintings, and jewelry are capturing the imagination of fans across the globe. Danita lives in México with her husband and daughter and delights in her ability to create joy through her art.

IMAGINED FLIGHT

Because what is "there" in real life for Danita isn't so pretty, she imagines what *could* be there in order to channel the inspiration she needs to create. "I live in a pretty common city … I dare say it is an ugly city … in a part of the country that is mostly sand," says Danita. Not present in this humble border town — officially located in the city of Juarez, Chihuahua, in México — are the plants and trees and vines that Danita yearns for. "I love all things green and I'd love to live in a forest or a jungle … a place full of green and living things and beauty all around," she says. "But this is where I live … and so I close my eyes and imagine a land with plants, trees, and lots of living things. This imagined land is what inspires me to create."

Dolls of all shapes
and sizes serve as
a huge source of
inspiration for Danita.
This passion is evident
in all that she creates,
which includes dolls
and other mixed-media
works that capture the
spirit of her fun and
playful personas.

Her colors
GREEN • BLUE • RED

"There's nothing more beautiful than a blue sky, a green land, and pretty flowers," says Danita. Which is why it is no surprise to learn that in fact her favorite color palette is green, blue, and red. "I think the palette works because we're familiar with the colors that are found in nature. I still haven't met a person who says, 'Look how beautiful the sky is today, all gray and full of smog.'"

Danita's imagination is not only green, but joyful, as evidenced by her art that is frequently described as being "happy." Danita explains that sometimes, she makes pieces to make people smile. "I hope that my work brings people joy, or evokes nice memories," says Danita. "Sometimes I want people to dream with me, to enter into a magical world where anything is possible. A world of dreams where you can fly … and believe."

MASTERFULLY MISMATCHED

The studio in which Danita creates her colorful artwork is a space she describes as her "refuge." "It is not the most beautiful or the biggest … but it's mine and I love to be there," says Danita. After having a baby, Danita and her husband decided to build an extra room to expand their humble two-bedroom house. Originally, the new addition was intended to become the larger master bedroom. "But things changed when I quit my day job to become a full-time mom and a nighttime artist. I needed more space. We realized that we only needed a bed and we only used the bedroom to sleep so we ended up moving into the smaller bedroom and allowed the larger add-on to become my studio.

The lush beauty of nature is what Danita often dreams of to gain inspiration needed to mix and juxtapose colors in her art as she aims to create a mood of cheerful and playful serenity.

She is inspired by ...

- Nature
- Frida Kahlo
- Hot baths
- Children's books
- Paper dolls
- Paintings by the masters — Matisse, Rothko, Picasso, Chagal, Kahlo, Botero, Tamayo, Lemieux, Meseroll, Cneut, Durand

"My studio has been built slowly, adding more furniture as needed ... which is why nothing matches," explains Danita. In order to bring some uniformity to the mismatched furniture pieces, Danita recruited her mom to help her make skirts for the tables, and also to paint the tables and add some pretty polka dotted papers. "My dad also helped me by installing a sink in one corner, which is one of the most useful things I have in the studio," says Danita.

Though not everything is perfect and it is always changing, the one true thing about Danita's studio is that it is filled with the things she loves. From art supplies to a collection of art dolls, to children's books and ephemera from around the world, Danita explains that "most of the things that I treasure and love are in my studio."

DOLLS, PAINTINGS & JEWELRY, OH MY!

The diversity of Danita's interests causes her to make an array of objects that are fast becoming objects of desire for collectors of art dolls, paintings, jewelry, and decorated boxes. "I usually have a hard time concentrating on one thing and get easily distracted," says Danita. "Right now I'm working mostly with acrylics. They are very versatile and the thing I like most about them is that they dry quick! And if they don't dry quickly enough, I have my heat gun ready to aid in the drying process."

Within the last year, Danita's body of work has made a splash in numerous publications including *Stuffed*, *Belle Armoire*, *Somerset Studio*, and *Art Doll Quarterly*. And on her popular Etsy site, fans can shop for all sorts of items including her acclaimed dolls, boxes, jewelry, pins, and art prints.

And true to her "distracted" nature of being, Danita is thinking of what's next for her, which may someday include pottery. "I love the smell of the clay and the feel of it," says Danita. "I also want to learn more about Photoshop®. I would love to make some digital versions of my original paintings."

She stays inspired

One of the first things Danita does when she is in a creative rut is clean. "It almost never fails," she says. "But cleaning my studio only … if I start cleaning the whole house it doesn't work. Maybe it's because I still am in contact with my materials when cleaning the studio."

Her Favorite Quote

Art is the only way to run away without leaving home.

— Twyla Tharp

Her tip for organization & exercise to fuel creativity

TIP: When creativity has to be interrupted in order to get up and search for materials, momentum can get lost. "Have what you use most within reach," says Danita. "My studio maybe is not the loveliest, but I have everything I need to work within arm's reach. I don't have to be standing up and searching for materials when I'm working."

Exercise: Close your eyes and imagine a place that you've always wanted to visit. With eyes closed, try hard to study the colors found in this place and notice all the different nuances of the shades and hues. Open your eyes and use the color palette from your imagination to create an art project.

She remembers

As a little girl, Danita loved to watch short TV segments interspersed in between regular cartoons called "Cositas" (Spanish for "little things"). "I remember watching the cartoons just to get to see the segments where they'd teach you about the 'project for the day,' along with all the materials needed to complete the project," she says. Danita's mom was very supportive by helping Danita gather all the materials needed in order for her to complete the projects presented on "Cositas."

Though Danita always loved art, she remembers being told by her kindergarten teacher that she had "scissor hands" and being chastised by her for "destroying" everything she touched. "I think I'm still trying to prove her wrong," says Danita.

FACING FEARS

Quitting a secure full-time office job to pursue what is becoming a very robust and successful career as an artist is a dream come true for Danita. But the act of making this happen was not easy. It was scary. But facing her fears and making it happen is in fact the essence of who Danita is … a woman who imagines possibilities to become who she seeks.

Another major fear that Danita overcame was her fear of dogs. "I used to be afraid even of little Chihuahuas," says Danita. But by facing this fear and actually getting an Old English Sheepdog to become part of her family, she was able to conquer her demons. "I've become a more secure person and an animal lover as well."

"We are all works in progress," says Danita. "And so is my studio. I like change and I'm always moving around my furniture and changing the state of things. The same happens with my art. I don't know if it's a bad or good thing, but it makes me feel good to have control over such things."

Danita is a mixed-media artist who lives in Juarez, Chihuahua, México. To learn more about Danita, visit www.danitaart.blogspot.com.

17

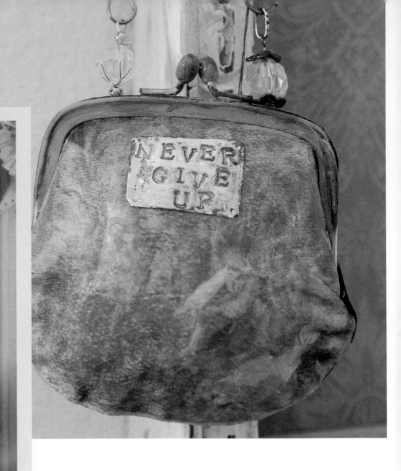

Connie Govea Stuart

With meticulous attention to detail, Connie Govea Stuart creates myriad lovelies from her home studio in northern California. From canvases to shrines to sewn objects to clay creations and more, Connie's works capture the tenderness and sweetness of her spirit and her dedication to making every day extraordinary.

ILLUMINATING DETAILS

The details and authenticity of life are what inspire Connie Govea Stuart. Connie's mother was one of the many people in her life who served as a role model for creativity and artistry. "As a painter, she became known for the details that she would put into her works … not the excesses, but the smallest of details … like the twinkle in an eye, a dimple, a wrinkle in a sleeve," she says. "I noticed all of her details and the details influenced me to value their presence … not only in art but in all facets of life."

Like many artists with a passion for vintage treasures, Connie is frequently found at antique shows and flea markets. But when she is on the hunt for treasures, it is really a hunt for details. "For example, the process of searching might lead me to an old key, but for me, it's less about the old key and more about the old key with the 'way-old' rim tag or numbered label on it. The details help me imagine more and with that imagination, prepare me to create in a more interesting manner."

To create custom scalloped edging for her studio hutch, Connie cuts assorted papers into scallop shapes and adheres them to the different levels of the hutch.

Perhaps it is because she appreciates details that she also appreciates good lighting. "Aside from nature's light, I have gathered only those light sources that are personally pleasing to look at," she says. "The older you get, the less 'things' you want … and instead the more you start investing in ways that can help you see with greater clarity, the details and blessings around you."

CREATING BEYOND SQUARE FOOTAGE

The one-bedroom townhouse that Connie currently shares with her beloved is not only completely their functional home but also completely Connie's creative space. "Where I create is humble, well-lit, and pretty simple," she says. "Sometimes I daydream about a separate place to do art. I keep sketches for what I have in mind and a vision for that sort of work area. However, where I create has never held me back. I can reach the best part of my creativity right here, and my current space serves me well."

When Connie started with her creative pursuits, her creative space was as large as a card table. Literally a wobbly, shaky, and unstable card table. On that table, Connie became one with her old black sewing machine. "I sewed and sewed and sewed heart-shaped lavender-stuffed sachets … all in different fabrics," she says. It is an experience that taught her that no matter how great or meager one's square footage is in terms of space, it is most important to be passionate and determined to create, despite the obstacles.

Her colors
CREAM • BEIGE • PUTTY
PARCHMENT • SAND

The color palette that Connie is most drawn to is a muted one, where the tones she uses include cream, beige, putty, parchment, and sand. This palette is a soothing and calming one, which is why her studio is infused with it. But in terms of creating art, Connie embraces the opportunity to play with brighter hues whenever possible.

THE ART OF LIVING

The mixed-media art that Connie creates is regularly featured in *Somerset Studio* and its many sister publications. But Connie is quick to point out that art isn't just about "official projects" that involve putting paint to canvas. Rather, art is anything that is born out of the passion and pride of making every facet of one's life extra special. "Whether it's a recipe, a sewing project, a wrapped gift … it's about the passion and pride in the artful making and presenting of anything … that's just part of who I am," she says. "Creating to me is so many things, including how we choose to see beauty in the details and finding ways to keep that beauty in your life."

Whether it's on a canvas or a box or a sewing project or more, Connie enjoys being inspired by collections. "I've been greatly influenced by collections," she says. "I've used objects that have inspired me for years, long before I knew the term 'mixed-media.' The elements are basic but I favor items that are seen beyond their intended use … and so I enjoy sharing them on canvas, in a case, or in a box. The best art piece for me to create is one that has to be opened to reveal a delightful surprise within."

Her tip for organization & exercise to fuel creativity

TIP: Especially because her creative space is a shared living space for Connie and her beau, she has made it a habit to put all of her supplies away each and every time she creates. This helps Connie clear her mind as she pulls it all out the next time she needs to create.

Exercise: Draw a flower from your imagination. Then go out and look at a flower and really study the details and then draw it. Compare how different the two flowers look.

She stays inspired

When Connie encounters a creative rut, she finds herself getting her groove back by making a heartfelt gift for someone in her life. "Everyone likes to receive happy mail that is unexpected and it always helps me get centered when I am able to create something that will lift up someone in my life," says Connie.

HAPPY AS A LARK

Future aspirations for Connie aren't as clear or important as the aspiration that she has for each and every day, which is to create warmth and beauty with authentic attention to details in her art and her relationships. And for now, Connie is happy as a lark not having to tend to a blog or Web site that might distract her from her primary agenda of tending to the beautiful details of life. After all, who wants to sit in front of the computer when there is a dimple to create in a heartfelt clay creation?

Connie Govea Stuart is a mixed-media artist who lives in northern California. She welcomes e-mails at connieart@aol.com.

She remembers

While her grandmother taught her to stitch intricate embroidery onto her pillowcases, Connie remembers her mom regularly stirring up clay concoctions from dough recipes for Connie to mold and paint. Aside from these regular interactions with the creative women in her family, Connie also remembers watching her dad demonstrate his own unique creative strength and dedication.

"My mom used to keep a picture of a sewing room she dreamed of … a vision that she tore out of a magazine. My dad used that picture and built the room for her, following through to make my mom's dream for her creative space come true."

Because many of Connie's art elements are tiny, vintage boxes with lots of small compartments are a must for her studio. They help Connie keep track of exactly what she needs for her various projects at hand.

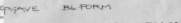

Hanne Matthiesen

With great thought and precision, Hanne Matthiesen prolifically creates multi-media works from her home in Denmark. To find inspiration, she rules nothing out from the world around her as she turns to words, books, nature, people, and experiences to help her create quilts, art books, and collages in a style that is beautifully minimalist and deliberate.

INTERNAL RESERVOIR

Topics and questions that are related to philosophical and existential matters are what most inspire Hanne Matthiesen. Such topics and questions frequently emerge in the form of words that ignite inspiration for Hanne to create. "It can be something I hear or read, but it can also be an image or something I see that looks interesting, and that makes me think," says Hanne. "When I say 'think' I don't mean the kind of deliberate thinking that one has to do during an exam … it's more a dream-like thinking … because if I think or focus too hard, the inspiration will slip away.

"Inspired creativity comes from both an internal reservoir of memories, impressions, feelings, hopes, dreams, and fears — as well as an external impulse in the form of a word, question, image, or experience. The point where the two meet is the point of ignition. There has to be both internal and external energy present. The amount of energy depends on whether I feel related to the subject. Does it reflect something I can relate to? If so, that's when creativity begins."

The color red is almost always present in Hanne's work. But she cautions that red needs to be used sparingly, as it is a color of power and strength — and when over-used on a project, it can become overpowering.

Natural light is one of Hanne's greatest sources of inspiration. Throughout the day, she follows the light by traveling from room to room, as she seeks to create where the presence of light is greatest.

LET THERE BE LIGHT

Daylight is another important source from which Hanne derives inspiration and energy. "I love daylight so usually I start my day in the kitchen or in my small studio — both of which are eastward and closely connected," says Hanne. "My small studio is a quite narrow room. It's mostly used for storing tools and materials as well as collections of collages and artists' books. But it's also here that I paint and glue … it's a bit messy but very inspiring." When she is in her kitchen, Hanne is usually writing. Articles, e-mails, workshop programs, business plans, and other documents that continue to grow are taken care of in her clean and simple kitchen. "But the kitchen table is also for working on collages and artists' books (especially when I run out of space at the studio table — which happens quite often)."

After the noon hour passes, Hanne follows the light to her westward studio and living room, where there is plenty of space and light. "The room is spacious enough to allow me to work on stuff that is too big for the table … like when I lay up a quilt or want to see how a collection of collages might appear, I often work on the floor of this room."

By following the light, Hanne utilizes most of her house and characterizes the various rooms in which she works as "creative zones." Says Hanne: "In the summer, I even use my terrace. It's a special pleasure to be working out in the open."

FRAGMENTS OF SIGNIFICANCE

Hanne started her art career by studying ceramics. But about 10 years ago, she switched her focus entirely to mixed-media works. "From my time with ceramics I've brought forward one chief trait: an interest in texture and surface, and a keen focus on the integration of elements and junctions into the unit," says Hanne.

"In my art, I am very concerned about the non-perfect, the beauty of decay, the fact that everything is in stages of change. In our culture, we sometimes seem to feel a little uneasy about the concept of decay. We prefer growth and flowering — not decay and death. But it is an equally essential part of the story, and it is a reminder for us to seize the day … and enjoy the journey."

In order to encourage her audience to appreciate the beauty of all of life's stages, Hanne tries to incorporate recycled and found objects in her work. She also likes to incorporate elements that appear outdated or are imperfect. "I love fragments from different realities, which I think help us become more inclusive of diversity," she adds.

Her colors
MUTED PASTELS • REDS • WHITES

"I fancy a Scandinavian palette with cool, dimmed, and muted shades of pastel colors and all kinds of white (e.g., broken white, off white, egg shell, cream, etc.) and a touch of pink or red," says Hanne. In place of pink or red, Hanne sometimes adds a bit of lime green. But this third color in her palette is added in very small doses. "My palette creates harmony and calmness," says Hanne. "By sticking to a limited scale of whites and muted pastels, bright colors can be refreshing — but also they quickly get very annoying. For me, being around colors that are too bright is like being surrounded by noise … which cause my senses to slow down and grow dull."

Her tips for organization & exercises to fuel creativity

TIP: Though they are pressure-filled, Hanne believes deadlines help you get started, keep you going, and help you structure time. "If nobody puts a task before you — make one yourself," she says.

Exercise: If you normally create at a table, make a change and create on the floor. Finding different spacial environments can affect your view of your work at hand.

TIP: To combat disorganization that can ensue when working alone, Hanne likes to involve herself with other artists to keep her on top of her game. Currently, she is involved with two art groups. "We meet frequently to discuss, exchange ideas and information, plan, work, exhibit, and even travel together. It's very inspirational," she says.

Exercise: Take a look at the books in a bookshelf and study the spines. Let random words and designs inspire your next creation.

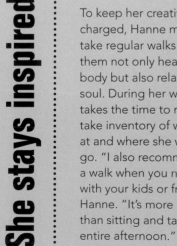

MAGIC OF LIFE

The fundamental reasons that motivate Hanne to make her art all boil down to large existential questions that most humans ask themselves: "Who am I?" and "What is the meaning of life?" Says Hanne: "I see my artwork as me reflecting on, and communicating these matters." And through her efforts, Hanne hopes that her work will inspire people to reflect on the magic of life, to see the beauty and poetic potential in the repeated rhythm of life, and to not be afraid to walk new roads along the journey of life.

"Life is magic, existence is a miracle. Every day the sun rises. It is a miracle. You open your eyes … it's a miracle. You breathe … your heart beats … and what have you done to make this happen? Nothing really, it's a gift somehow. And we are all part of it. We are universal beings, world citizens, and individual personalities … a sort of 'extended family.'"

Hanne Matthiesen is a mixed-media artist who lives in Denmark. To learn more about her art and life, visit www.ihanne.wordpress.com.

She remembers

As a child, Hanne lived in a small village in the countryside, next to a schoolyard. "The whole yard was covered with a layer of fine pebbles. In the center towered an enormous chestnut tree," says Hanne. "Near the schoolyard was a small public lawn framed by a row of rosebushes. Somebody got the idea of using the buds as 'brushes' or 'pens' and we all started to 'draw' on the pavement … this is when I felt I had discovered a magical universe where patterns could be made directly on the ground."

She stays inspired

To keep her creative energies charged, Hanne makes sure to take regular walks. She finds them not only healthy for the body but also relaxing for the soul. During her walks, Hanne takes the time to reflect and take inventory of where she is at and where she would like to go. "I also recommend taking a walk when you need to talk with your kids or friends," says Hanne. "It's more relaxing than sitting and talking for an entire afternoon."

HAUNTING QUALITY

What Ashley Carter is inspired by doesn't fit into a nutshell. "I'm inspired by fairy tales, folklore, deeply southern traditions, superstitions, vintage carnival, theater, and circus ephemera, and my mother's style of entertaining," she says. "And if I weren't in charge of everything related to Goldbug Studio, I'd probably be renovating houses or creating theater and movie sets."

Aside from all of these fantastic sources of inspiration, Ashley also turns to New Orleans as a clear and present muse within her work. "My work has been heavily inspired by my childhood memories and impressions of New Orleans," she says. "My paternal grandmother, Meme, lived uptown on Napoleon Avenue for over 50 years. I was born in New Orleans and my family visited often … I've always thought of that city as a storybook place — almost like visiting a foreign country. I remember feeling slightly stunned when a buyer at my first wholesale show said my pieces reminded her of Mardi Gras floats. Until that moment, I hadn't consciously made the connection."

Ashley Carter

Ashley Carter uses her fascination with fantasy and fairy tales to design inspired creations that help people celebrate life. To get her designs produced and out into the world, she oversees a production staff through her company called Goldbug Studio, where each and every piece is lovingly handmade in Raleigh, North Carolina.

When Ashley embarks on creating one of her signature pieces, she leaves no stone unturned in terms of materials used. Branches, leaves, vintage millinery, and found objects are fair game — and always abundantly present in her studio.

The final source of major inspiration for Ashley is what she describes as "hauntings." "Most members of my family believe that my grandmother's home in New Orleans and my family's first home in Greensboro, North Carolina, were both haunted," she says. For Ashley, the idea that a house or object could be haunted is absolutely fascinating to her. "The creepier the better," she says. "I like using vintage elements in my designs and giving them new life … I've been told many times that there is a haunted quality to some of my work."

VINTAGE MILLINERY FOUND

In 2003 when Ken and Carolyn Blazier (Ashley's largest millinery supplier) were ready to retire, Ashley took one look at their inventory in Georgia and purchased the entire inventory. She knew it would be a once-in-a-lifetime opportunity. To house it all, Ashley found a warehouse space outside her home to make it all come together. "Originally, it was just a raw warehouse space … but it had an amazing arched wood-frame ceiling and good natural light," she says. "The studio is shotgun style — a long narrow space about 650 square feet with painted concrete floors … the space is cheery, light, and bright with French blue porcelain enamel light fixtures, a vintage crystal chandelier, 1940s wallpaper, and vintage furniture."

While the production team for Goldbug Studio works on a long communal counter created with stained doors facing two huge picture windows and a fenced courtyard, Ashley's personal studio space is separated from the main production line by a partition wall. "I prefer to do most of my work on the counter in the main studio but when I need to really concentrate or spread all of my junk everywhere, my private studio is a great refuge," she says.

HANDMADE FOLLIES

The art that Ashley regularly designs for Goldbug Studio is a collection of sparkling handmade follies, fairy tale-inspired figures, decadent headpieces, and vintage-style party embellishments. The process of constructing her designs into products can be described as "vintage mixed-media" where paper sculptures are blended with vintage millinery elements and carefully selected vintage embellishments.

"My designs wed the simple and the extravagant," says Ashley. "I'm not a purist. I'm not interested in trying to re-create pieces from a specific era — I like to mix it all up. For example, I'll use 1930s pageant queen paper dolls and Victorian starlets mixed with 1950s wallpaper, glass glitter candies, vintage crepe paper, 1920s millinery, and new wired French ribbon candy."

Though many things in Ashley's collection have a muted vintage aesthetic, she likes to mix such findings with modern-day elements like glass glitter, glossy papers, and colorful fabrics and embellishments.

Her colors

ROBIN'S EGG BLUE • SEA GREEN • IVORY

Ashley's favorite color palette is made up of robin's egg blue, sea green, and ivory. "It's a lovely, calm, and serene palette," she says. "I need to live with light colors, big windows, and open space. I like a pop of red or black here and there for drama and interest but in general, I live in a sun-dappled blue-green world."

With the endless demands of running a business, Ashley sometimes finds herself battling creative ruts. "I get overwhelmed with the business end of things and before I know it, a few weeks can pass without much time spent in the studio," she says. As soon as Ashley becomes aware of this, she will make sure, after her staff members leave for the day, to put on one of her all-time favorite movies, turn off the phone, and start moving her hands in her studio. When this happens, a new piece will usually start to form — often around 2:00 a.m.

Her tip for organization & exercise to fuel creativity

TIP: Ashley Carter knows a thing or two about design and assembly. For keeping things organized during production, Ashley recommends that all elements be pulled together and meticulously counted. "Prep all parts in a systematic way … by cutting everything at once, spraying everything at once, and glittering all at once. Once all the prep is done, and you're sure you have everything you need to complete the project, you can assemble," she says.

Exercise: Over-valuing vintage finds can inhibit creativity. The next time you feel such inhibition, consider taking a prized vintage treasure and creating something with it. By using an item that you've been afraid to use because you might not find another one just like it, you'll be surprised that even more extraordinary things will enter your life, now that you've made room for them.

CELEBRATING LIFE

Each piece offered through Goldbug Studio is handmade in Raleigh, North Carolina. Among the large collection of designs, birds and other wired creations have become Goldbug Studio's signature. It's important to Ashley that her designs look like they have moving parts, as they are inspired by her love of fantasy and fairy tales that are — in our imaginations — never stagnant but very much full of motion and life. "The Goldbug Studio Collection is a culmination of all the stories, characters, and elaborate parties that live in my head," she says.

In many ways, what Ashley creates are works that help people celebrate. She remembers that a collector once described one of her crown designs as "the birthday cake I never had." And for an artist whose mission is to create celebratory magic inspired by fantasies and fairy tales, Ashley took the collector's comments as the "ultimate compliment." "It's a celebration of childhood, imagination, and life," she says.

Ashley Carter is proprietor of Goldbug Studio, where she designs and assembles elegant adornments for the home and special occasions. To learn more, visit www.goldbugstudio.com.

She remembers

Ashley remembers growing up with a very generous father who interestingly hated receiving gifts that were fancy or expensive. "Fancy cars, designer labels, the latest gadgets ... these things have never motivated him in his career or his life," she says. "He was always happiest with a handmade gift from one of his four girls. I learned very early on that a simple gift made of Popsicle sticks from one of his four daughters would bring him more joy than a Polo shirt." This type of handmade upbringing was cultivated by both her father and mother — resulting in a family that values the art of making and giving heartfelt gifts by hand.

INSPIRED DETAILS

Flea markets and the treasures that abound there are a huge source of inspiration for Lori. "When I walk through my favorite flea market or antique store, I'm inspired by the details," says Lori. "Like a crumpled piece of paper that has the most beautiful penmanship … or an old sewing box filled with old buttons and tangled seam binding. Such elements immediately trigger visions of projects in my head."

The small creative space in her home is where Lori houses many of her vintage findings. And every time she walks into her creative space, she is able to discover again and again the magic of assorted items that she has lovingly collected over the years. "I feel very inspired to see an old piece of tattered lace popping out from the shoe caddy or a lush bloom that I pinned up on my inspiration board," she says.

Aside from flea markets and the findings from such jaunts that she has stored in her creative space, Lori keeps her eyes wide open for inspiration that can come from unexpected places — like when she and her family were vacationing in Michigan and driving along a road. "While we were driving, I saw an old bicycle on the side of the road with the most beautiful red roses growing out of the wicker basket," she explains. "I screamed and told my husband to turn around so I could take a photo of it. When I came home from vacation, I created a collage with red roses — just like the ones I saw in the basket."

Lori Oles

Vintage Flair isn't just the name of Lori Oles' blog … it is the inspirational mantra of her artwork and life. Lori lovingly collects vintage papers and ephemera to create works that are regularly featured in *Somerset Life* magazine and her very popular artful blog. She lives in Fayetteville, Arkansas, with her husband and three children.

To make the most of her small space, Lori uses fabric shoe organizers to store her art materials. She also uses clothespins to attach items to the fronts of each pocket to make the them look inviting.

CLEVER SOLUTIONS

Finding clever solutions to small spaces has always been Lori's forté. In fact, her very first craft "space" was a trio of old trunks that Lori stored in her family room. "I used them to store my craft supplies and every time I created my art, I would take the trunks to the kitchen table to get my portable studio set up," she says.

Eventually, Lori's need for space became much larger than could be held in those trunks. Her current space is now a walk-in closet located under the stairs near her kitchen that she and her husband were able to transform into a studio. "To make the most out of the space, my husband built a desk area to maximize the awkward low ceiling," she explains. "By doing that, it also created a lot of storage underneath the desk and that is where I keep my actual art supplies like scissors, glue guns, glitter, paints, brushes, and stamps … all in large plastic file cabinets. I then used my staple gun to add the yellow toile fabric skirt to cover the unsightly but necessary storage."

One essential storage element that helps Lori keep things beautifully stored without taking up a lot of space is the fabric shoe organizer. "I actually have two of them in the studio … one is a vintage bark cloth organizer and it hangs on the wall," she says. "I use that one to store scraps of paper from past projects, cards, feathers, wallpaper, and old invoices. I love how each pocket has something interesting popping out of the pocket just waiting to be used."

With three children, a husband, a cat, and a dog, Lori continues to find solutions to optimize the space that is available to create. Though her studio is small, Lori points out with great pride that it is packed to the brim with beauty and inspiration.

By using bulletin boards, boxes, and shelves, Lori maximizes every inch of her space, which is a walk-in closet located under the stairs near her kitchen.

SELF-TAUGHT PASSION

Lori is a self-taught artist who is passionate about creating almost anything that incorporates vintage paper. "My favorite papers are found in old ledgers," says Lori. "I am amazed at the beautiful penmanship and patina on the pages. I never tire of creating collages and I think that is my absolute favorite thing to make."

There are actually three signature elements that Lori finds irresistible when she creates collage work: old millinery flowers, tattered pieces of crocheted trim, and vintage papers. Fans of Lori's work would argue that it isn't just a collage that she makes. She in fact infuses every facet of her life with lovely details. Whether it's packing a picnic, preparing a place setting, or embellishing a storage unit, it is the art of life that Lori is able to create.

Her tips for organization & exercises to fuel creativity

TIP: When Lori finishes a project, she puts everything back in its rightful place. "If you don't follow this simple rule, you'll regret it because your studio will quickly become a mess," she cautions.

Exercise: Whatever your favorite color palette may be, add some shimmer by adding foil or metallic paint or jewelry pieces. You'll be surprised at how the palette transforms.

TIP: Rather than storing treasures in boxes, Lori keeps everything out and visible. "As a visual person, I'm afraid I wouldn't get much done if I had to open a bunch of boxes and dig through to find hidden supplies," she says.

Exercise: If the thought of a large project is intimidating, try making the project first in miniscule form. Once you allow yourself to make it in small scale, you can tackle the larger-scale project.

When Lori finds special vintage clothing items, she likes to place them on pretty hangers and display them near her windows so that they become part of her home and studio décor.

NEW FRONTIERS

Being called an "artist" is something that Lori is still getting used to. "I have never been formally trained in art," she explains. "I just think of myself as a really crafty type of person. I am somewhat taken aback when people leave lovely comments on my blog on how I have inspired them."

Through her self-taught expressions of art, Lori hopes that her audience will experience a sense of softness and romance. Lori also hopes to pursue more use of paint and is currently reading books on different techniques that she would like to try. "I would also like to be more spontaneous with my art and capture the moment by drawing or doodling in my art journals," she says. Whether it's painting or art journaling, Lori will undoubtedly pursue all new art frontiers with "unofficial" training but a most official attention to detail.

Lori Oles is a mixed-media artist whose work is frequently published in Somerset Life *magazine. To learn more about her art and life, visit* www.vintageflair.typepad.com.

She remembers

The earliest memory of creativity that Lori has is sneaking into her mom's sewing room as a little girl to quietly cut pieces from her mom's stash of fabrics. "I used these cut fabrics to create blankets for my dollhouse," says Lori. "I also remember collecting toothpaste caps to use as vases for the dollhouse."

UNIFYING THREAD

Vickie Howell is inspired by pop culture. And for as long as she can remember, she's been observing how very much we are all connected by the way we experience pop culture. From TV shows to movies, from music to toys, from fast-food restaurants to current events and more, Vickie is fascinated at how through the process of *life* happening, *we* also "happen" in our unique ways, and through our unique lenses. "There is a unifying thread to it all," she says.

"For me, pop culture is another way of documenting history. You may not remember the exact date a historical event happened, but if you say 'Cuckoo for Cocoa Puffs,' or download the song 'Rock Lobster' on iTunes, those popular icons will take you to a place in history and ignite unique feelings and emotions. I believe that pop culture is how we as human beings bond with one another."

Vickie's recent book titled *Pop Goes Crochet* (Lark, 2009) capitalizes on this phenomenon as she offers an array of projects inspired by celebrities and current events. "I'm always observing commercials and TV shows or listening to music," she says. And what might be some of her faves when it comes to TV shows? "I love *The Office*, *Big Love*, *Mad Men*, and … I love shows that have a little sarcasm and wit to them."

Vickie Howell

Vickie Howell is a master crafter of community. It is a community of understanding that she hopes to perpetuate through her passion for knitting and crocheting, as expressed through her books, TV shows, Web site, and licensed products. She makes all of it happen in Austin, Texas, where she lives with an ever-growing stash of yarn, needles and hooks, along with a husband and children who all "get it."

Vickie loves collecting knitting needles of all shapes, colors, and sizes and prominently displaying them in her studio.

Vickie embraces the challenge of working with diverse color palettes that she can manipulate to have projects yield looks that are either classic, quirky, or vintage.

THE "KOFFICE"

Aside from pop culture, Vickie names her husband and children as her main source for inspiration. And it is through their generous support and love that Vickie is able to keep the pedal to the metal with all of her endeavors, which happen in her hybrid kitchen-turned-studio that is endearingly referred to as her "koffice."

"It's a really good-sized kitchen," she says. "The largest part of the house, really … with a big worktable, shelves, and a desk. Having this koffice is a blessing and a curse because when you work at home, you can't shut it off. You stare at everything all the time. And you never feel you have the license to stop working."

As an avid knitter and crocheter, Vickie notes that her art can easily travel. That is, she doesn't necessarily have to be in her koffice in order to create with her yarn, needles, and hooks. She can knit in the car, at the park, on the soccer field. However, with her growing popularity, Vickie states that a large part of what she spends her time on isn't just creating art but creating the publicity and business infrastructure to support her art. "It's not as glamorous as people might think," she says. "When I first got the TV show [*Knitty Gritty*], I had craft supplies everywhere. The life of an artist goes through 'feast and famine' phases, and so being relentless and never letting up on keeping yourself out there is very important. And if you are an artist with kids and you want to participate in your children's lives, then you really have to make it all happen in your home."

Her colors

BLACK • TURQUOISE CHARTREUSE • ORANGE

Had it not been for knitting, Vickie doubts that she would have discovered colors at all. "I would have been comfortable living in black," she says. But knitting with black yarn isn't that great on the eyes, which is why she started knitting with colors in the first place. The combination of turquoise, chartreuse, and orange (with black) together represent a retro-inspired palette that works for Vickie.

ART THAT RESONATES

Whether it's through her books or TV show or magazine articles or the Web content that she produces, Vickie believes that what she is meant to do as a creative soul is to perpetuate community. "I have been fortunate enough to have a voice and a platform … I really feel it is such a gift to make a living doing what you love … it instills in me a responsibility to perpetuate that passion for creativity," she says.

"In particular, I hope that my work can resonate with kids and help them see the common bond we all share … and to know that we are not all that different from one another. I find that kids are able to obtain joy from nominal things that I may not have considered." When she observes her own kids, Tanner and Tristan, making objects out of humble mediums — like paper plate skeletons — she is always struck to see that they don't care so much about the ordinariness of their supplies, but the extraordinariness of the process. "There's value in 'having a ball' during the creative process … which kids have a special knack for doing."

Her tips for organization & exercises to fuel creativity

TIP: Vickie swears by clear containers and wire baskets for storing her supplies. "If you can't see it, you won't remember that you have it," she says.

Exercise: Think about your favorite commercial and create a project inspired by it.

TIP: Another item that helps Vickie stay organized is a label maker. She uses hers to label her containers, baskets, folders, and more, to help her remember exactly what each cluster of items is intended for.

Exercise: Turn on a favorite playlist that you are very familiar with and try to start and finish a project before the entire playlist rotates through.

Because the demands for keeping all of her projects remain consistently intense, Vickie doesn't ever find herself in a creative rut. "There's no time to be in a rut, really. I never stop," she says. "This is not to say that I probably need to find ways to recharge and regroup but I'm not good at taking a step back and taking care of myself. I'm never not thinking about my work and all the 'next' things I need to take care of."

Vickie surrounds herself with clippings from magazines and catalogs, along with fun fabric samples that help inspire her designs.

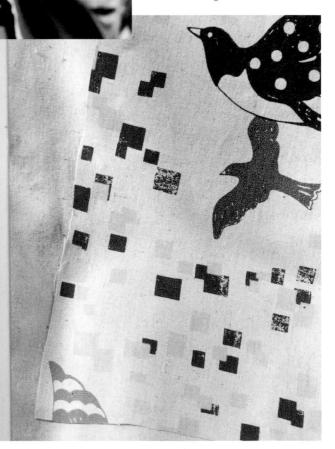

ADDED BLESSINGS

Blessed is Vickie as her greatest source of inspiration — her family — has grown as she and her husband just recently welcomed the birth of their daughter, Clover. Like Vickie's sons, Tanner and Tristan, Clover will most certainly become someone who interprets pop culture in her own unique way … a way that Vickie will observe closely and be inspired by deeply as she continues on her journey to perpetuate a community of art and love.

Vickie Howell is host of the DIY TV show Knitty Gritty *and author of numerous knitting and crocheting books, including* Pop Goes Crochet *and* AwareKnits™ (Lark, 2009). *To learn more, visit* www.vickiehowell.com.

She remembers

"I actually don't remember a time when there wasn't crafting in my life," says Vickie. "As soon as I could hold a glue stick, I was making things." One of her fondest memories of this creativity that has always been in her life is when she and her best friend from childhood used Popsicle sticks and paper to create "stop" and "go" signs to use as they played "traffic cop."

Amy Hanna

Amy Hanna designs one-of-a-kind jewelry that is nothing short of exceptional. She lovingly shepherds each vintage element that she collects from all over the world to compose transformative pieces that evoke history, beauty, and artistry.

SOUND OF SILENCE

As a mother of three young children, silence is a valuable and rare commodity for Amy Hanna. With birthday parties, carpooling, homework supervision, and other everyday demands that she juggles at the speed of light, things can get pretty … well … loud.

Perhaps it is because silence is so rare that Amy finds complete silence — coupled with her deep connection with God — to be her main source of inspiration when she creates. "After saying a quick prayer before getting started, I love the feeling of being overtaken by creativity … where my hands cannot move fast enough and my mind dances with ideas," says Amy. "I find myself working in complete silence except for the noise that comes from my old industrial clock that hangs above me."

Aside from the sound of silence, Amy is inspired by antique stores, flea markets, sandy beaches, and really good stories. "Treasures I encounter at stores and markets become that much more valuable when there is a story behind them," says Amy. And once she learns of those stories, inspiration becomes almost unstoppable as Amy integrates old elements into new objects with reinvented destinies.

Amy Hanna is passionate about presenting her work with an aesthetic that is congruent to her jewelry designs. A vintage religious Santos with perfectly weathered paint is a perfect example of the kind of inspired presentation that Amy values.

She is inspired by ...

- Complete silence
- Sandy beaches
- Flea markets
- Antique stores
- Good stories

GRANNY'S CLOSET

As a little girl, Amy loved to visit her granny's famous toy closet. "From the moment I walked into her walk-in closet, my eyes were wide open absorbing all the old games, dolls, and trinkets that were displayed on the many shelves. There was something special about that closet that stayed close to my heart," says Amy.

Perhaps it is this fond memory of her granny's closet that makes Amy especially connected to the closet within the spare bedroom in her home that is now her art studio. "I have always felt your closet should be a special place that stores special things," says Amy. "I guess that is why when we moved into our current home the first thing I did to the room that would become my studio was to remove the closet doors and install shelves."

She stays inspired

It is no wonder that before embarking on any creative project that Amy Hanna — a woman of tremendous faith — begins everything with a prayer. "I always say a quick prayer before I get started," she says. Amy also reads one of her favorite scriptures (Ephesians 6:18), which is written on a chalkboard hanging on the door of her studio to help her mind and spirit get properly prepared for the task at hand.

REJUVENATED JEWELS

Indeed, it is this closet that holds baskets full of very special objects that Amy has collected over the years. And it is this closet that remains open and inviting as Amy regularly enters her studio to settle next to it and under a vintage chandelier where she can create her one-of-a-kind jewelry.

It is a special knack that Amy has for taking vintage treasures and creating new designs with them ... a process that she teaches and illustrates in her much anticipated book titled *Rejuvenated Jewels* (Quarry, 2009). "I usually work with silver, pearls, wire, rhinestones, brass, religious pieces, and vintage souvenirs," says Amy. And what she hopes in the process of making her jewelry is that the works will cause people to feel a connection with the past. And that stories from the past can mingle with elements from the present to give birth to brand new stories ... rejuvenated ones.

Her colors
MERCURY • FRENCH BLUES • GRAYS • LINENS

Amy's favorite color palette is always evolving but there are a handful of colors that she is drawn to time and time again. "I am drawn to French blues and grays mixed with linen," says Amy. Aged mercury is also part of her palette, which adds a nice touch of shimmer to all that she creates.

Her Favorite Quote

She is more precious than rubies: and all the things thou canst desire are not to be compared unto her.

— Proverbs 3:15

She remembers

Being an only child helped Amy reach deep into her imagination to keep herself entertained. "I remember having a very vivid imagination," says Amy. "Which is part of the reason I saw things differently than most other people." Growing up, Amy was surrounded by very creative people who taught Amy not to be afraid to take chances and to use her hands. Her grandmother taught her to take great pride in things made by hand.

Amy Hanna is a jewelry and mixed-media artist who lives in southern California. She is the author of Rejuvenated Jewels (Quarry, 2009). *To learn more about Amy Hanna, visit* www.amyhanna.typepad.com.

DESIGNING EXCEPTIONAL

Amy's down-to-earth ways might cause fans to believe that what she does is easy. But no matter the silence or beautiful surroundings, Amy can't escape the very hard work involved with making all of it happen.

But hard work has never stopped Amy. At the age of 18, she moved out of her home to find her own way. "Eventually creating a home with my husband across the country and away from the rest of my own family has been a challenge," says Amy. "And for the past year, putting myself out there to write my first book while tending to my children and all of the other life demands has been no easy feat.

"I am really inspired by people who work really hard to achieve their dreams," she says. Which explains why she herself works so hard, and never accepts anything that falls short of exceptional."

Vintage velvet boxes are abundantly present in Amy's studio, where she stores her prized vintage elements.

Bonzie

Bonzie creates achingly beautiful garments and accessories in the enchanting land of Ireland. She works in collaboration with Ger — her beloved auntie and sewing partner for her independent clothing label that continues to gain popularity amongst fashion and artwear enthusiasts from around the globe.

OLDE WORLDE INSPIRATION

Sometimes, Bonzie wonders whether she has lived a past life. This is because she is passionately drawn to an era of old. "I tend to be drawn to items and surfaces that display the passage of time," says Bonzie. "I have a real affinity with days gone by and olde worlde things. I am drawn to and inspired by how a gate has tarnished over the years, an antique chair with its under padding poking out of its threadbare corners." Such items from the past cause Bonzie to imagine a lost world of romance and mystery.

Another source of inspiration for Bonzie is music. "A song can sound like fabric to me," she explains. "I can be listening to something and think to myself, 'That sounds like leather strapping over whispy tulle.' A song can evoke a mood, the mood can then evoke a design … it's a cumulative process." Songs from musicals and soundtracks from movies are some of Bonzie's favorites. "I also adore Imogen Heap, Evanescence, and works by composer Michael Nyman," says Bonzie.

Bonzie loves to prominently display some of her
favorite pieces from her collection in her studio.
Capelets are hung along a window, scarves are draped
on a dressform, and jackets are hung along shelving
units. They beautify the space, and inspire the artist.

ANTIQUE CREAM • SMOKY GRAY • JET BLACK

In her never-ending pursuit to create a mood of subdued elegance, Bonzie is drawn to a color palette made up of antique cream, smoky gray, and jet black. "I love monochromatic color schemes," she says. "I like to think that this palette creates drama, vintage romance, and of course a little bit of haunted romanticism."

Whether it's antiques or music soundtracks, Bonzie surrounds herself with many elements from sources that inspire her. "And subconsciously I pick up elements that I am drawn to," says Bonzie. "When left to be with my own thoughts, my imagination will always veer toward fantasy and fairy tales. It's often during these daydreams that tomorrow's piece will emerge."

FAVORITE ESCAPE

When Bonzie and her partner, Tony, moved into their new home, they also purchased a wooden cabin-like structure that has become her studio. "I had always lived in apartments … and fabrics and textiles took over any space I ever occupied," says Bonzie. "I knew my partner wouldn't enjoy living with that much lace so we decided to give my work a home of its own."

During her days as a college student at the National College of Art and Design in Dublin, Bonzie was enamored and blessed with the abundance of sewing accoutrements and pattern-cutting tables made available through the studio spaces on campus. "There were even designated areas for design work up on a balcony area, and downstairs housed huge cutting tables surrounded by banks of sewing machines and tailoring dummies." When she finished her studies and moved into her first apartment, she became humbled to meet the real world — one that was devoid of the kind of space and equipment that she had become accustomed to as a design student in college.

Bonzie works with her sewing partner, Ger, who also happens to be her auntie. Together, they create the pieces that make up the collection for their independent fashion label, based in Ireland.

57

She is inspired by ...

- The past
- Silence
- Worn & faded furniture
- Music

Her current studio is one that she shares with her sewing partner, Ger, who also happens to be Bonzie's auntie. Both Bonzie and Ger consider the studio a favorite escape. "To be honest, I spend an unhealthy amount of time there," says Bonzie. "My favorite piece in the studio is a large handmade cutting table that was lovingly made by my father and little brother. It reminds me daily of their support, which I am so grateful to have."

Her tips for organization & exercises to fuel creativity

TIP: By storing her supplies and materials according to color, Bonzie is able to find everything she needs for a project right away. "All the lace is in its own basket sectioned into color schemes, as is the case with the tulle, the beading fabric, and so on," says Bonzie.

Exercise: Select a favorite character from a musical that you like and create a piece of art that you think would suit the character.

TIP: When a project is near-finished, Bonzie likes to keep it and all related parts in one open basket. "Keeping everything related to that particular piece together makes it easy to come back to at a later time, when you are ready to finish it," she says.

Exercise: After working on a project, add a sheer layer on top of it with a piece of tulle or vellum or netting to see how the project takes on a different effect.

FADED GRANDEUR

Artistic clothing and accessories are what Bonzie and Ger create. "We work together on our independent Irish design label by creating clothing with a distinctive romantic vintage vibe," says Bonzie. "I would describe our work as 'Corpse Bride weds Phantom of the Opera' and hope that this would conjure up images of faded grandeur."

The client base for Bonzie and Ger's independent design has captured the imaginations of people not only in Ireland but also in the United States. Bonzie's design aesthetic is also described as "tattered couture" and for the past year, Bonzie has shared her aesthetic on a regular basis as a columnist for "Tattered Couture" in Stampington & Company's *Belle Armoire* magazine.

Olde worlde fabrics, thrifted trinkets, lace, silks, velvet, and opulent adornments are what Bonzie and Ger use in their designs. By using such fineries, Bonzie hopes that her work brings a little fantasy and escapism for the wearer. "It's lovely to know that our pieces have the power to create a little romantic daydreaming," says Bonzie. "This is especially true of our bridal clients."

She stays inspired

For Bonzie, the glass of water is never half empty. It's always half full. And her optimistic spirit about art and life is evident in the joyous works she creates. But even optimists like Bonzie experience creative ruts. "If I have one of those days, I need to enlist a bit of escapism to the movie theater," says Bonzie. "Usually the reason for a creative block is something in our personal lives pulling on our energies. I find a good movie helps to clear the head of too much worrying."

Clear jars are must-have storage units for Bonzie. She uses them to store fabrics and ribbons according to color. For tools and materials that she doesn't actively need, she uses containers according to size.

CRYSTALLIZED INDEPENDENCE

The one life experience that crystallized Bonzie's commitment to pursue the development of an independent label was during an internship she had with a designer in Paris, France. "The whole experience was extremely difficult … long hours, tough living expenses, scary late nights along the metro," recalls Bonzie.

"But I wouldn't change that experience one bit. It was one of those life-shaping experiences where I learned a lot about the type of person I am and where I learned that I would like to be in the fashion industry. I gathered insight into the way things work and recognized that I was particularly fond of creating a small independent label that would allow a level of personal touch and intimacy between designer and client."

Bonzie creates artistic clothing and accessories in Ireland. She is a regular columnist for Belle Armoire *magazine. To learn more about her work, visit her Web site at* www.bonziedesigns.com *or her blog at* www.designsbybonzie.blogspot.com.

She remembers

One of Bonzie's earliest artistic memories is with her beloved nana. "She used to spend time with me when I was a little girl, watching me as I colored on the backsides of cereal packets. She always made a big deal of my drawings … it was a wonderful bonding experience," says Bonzie. "My father was also a huge creative catalyst. We spent a lot of time drawing together."

IN LIVING COLOR

People who love Pam Garrison's art are people who love color. Whether it's on the pages of her art journals, or her various mixed-media projects, or her lovely blog posts, Pam drenches everything she creates with stunning colors. "Colors and color combinations really spark my creative juices," says Pam. "I never know when my love of a certain color will hit … it changes with time. People often comment about my use of color as something they like about my art, which makes me feel good … that maybe I can spread creative inspiration through my use of colors and color combinations."

Another source of inspiration for Pam is flea markets. She's been to plenty of them over the years, and never tires of making a trek to the next flea marketing opportunity where she can search for assorted treasures. "I absolutely love the hunt … sometimes as much as the creating … finding someone's unwanted bits and seeing the potential they hold is very exciting and stimulating, and gets my wheels spinning," says Pam. Not surprisingly, items that she gravitates toward during these jaunts are in fact items with the kinds of beautiful colors and color combinations that she loves and is inspired by. "I love the unpacking of my finds once home. It is so fun to clean them up, admire their colors, reorganize them, and put them to use," says Pam.

In order to add visual interest and a focal frame to certain parts of her studio, Pam likes to strategically attach sheets of vintage journal pages to portions of her wall.

Pam enjoys projects like embroidery samplers because they have no rules or set structure. She enjoys creating and practicing various stitches on plain muslin — much like her doodling process where she simply allows herself to meander on the page or fabric with experimental designs.

STUDIO IN PROGRESS

The home that Pam and her family live in is one that they moved into just a year ago. And the space that Pam calls her studio is an extra bedroom on the second floor of the house, where she keeps all of her papers, findings, fabrics, sewing machine, art journals, paints, pens, and so much more that she uses to create her magic. "My studio is a work-in-progress," says Pam. "The time I've lived here has flown by, with only a few studio projects being completed. The wallpapered closet was a pretty big project, and getting the cupboards hung; even the process of cleaning up in general felt like a big accomplishment!"

As a wife and mother of two, Pam finds that even with a studio space of her own, she finds herself creating in different parts of the house so that she can be closer to her family. "Even though I have all my supplies in my studio, I often find myself loading supplies up and bringing them downstairs so I can be involved with my family at the same time," says Pam. "I usually have a few different projects in a basket or two in the family room, and often work at the kitchen table while working with the kids on homework." But when the kids are in school or when everyone is in bed, Pam is back in her studio to enjoy the stillness and quiet of the entire house, which helps her focus on her creations.

Her tip for organization & exercise to fuel creativity

TIP: Pam recommends that even with the smallest of objects, it's important to give them a home so that when things get disheveled, it is easy to put things back into their proper place.

Exercise: Grab a piece of plain fabric, needle, and embroidery thread. Don't think about an overall design. Just allow yourself to create small "doodles" as you would on paper by stitching small experimental patterns and designs.

Her colors
SHADES OF WHITE & CREAM

As one who draws inspiration first and foremost from colors and color combinations, Pam finds the shades of white and cream to be her color palette of choice. "I fall in and out of other colors, but my love for creams is constant," says Pam.

MASTER OF MAGIC

There are many things that Pam is good at, and therefore many things that she is able to create. "I love to journal, sew, collage … I am largely drawn to paper, fabric, and small little embellishment items," says Pam. "My primary tools are paper, pens (including ink and dip pens), a needle, thread, scissors, and any sewing machine."

The small embellishments and tiny details are what Pam is very attuned to with whatever she creates, which is part of the reason people are so drawn to her work. The doodles and flourishes in her art journal pages are frequently studied by fans who seek to emulate her playful style. The combination of colors that she is able to hit so well in her mixed-media works are also a source of great inspiration for fans of her work.

And the magic she's able to make with papers and pens is something she can also create with fabrics, needle, and thread. On the horizon for Pam is always finding new techniques and mediums she wants to try. "I'd like to try my hand at so many things in the future," says Pam. "Rug hooking, graphic arts, print making, sewing little stuffed or chenille animals … it's an ever-expanding list."

Creative ruts are a rarity for Pam. With the demands of life tugging at her at various angles, she is usually thirsty to get into her studio to create. "I'm usually chomping at the bit to get to something, so the minute I have a free moment to do so, I just jump right in," says Pam. "Not many ruts to combat when you feel you don't have enough time to create."

FROM THE HEART

If there is anything central to Pam's artwork, many would say it is the love she has for her family. Pam loves to create one-of-a-kind items that celebrate milestones for her son, daughter, and husband. The love she passes onto her family through the art she creates from her heart parallels the love she received from her own family — especially from her artistic and creative parents.

At the age of 16, Pam sorrowfully said good-bye to her mother who passed away after having suffered from a long bout of cancer. "I find that when I take classes and we have some assigned project, the loss of my mother or love for her ends up surfacing somewhere within the project and it surprises me that it does," says Pam. "I guess the whole experience is always on my heart more than I realize. That doesn't mean that all my art is full of deep hidden meanings. Sometimes it's just wonderful when I feel that people 'get' what I make and understand why I might want to make it."

Pam Garrison is a mixed-media artist who lives in southern California. To learn more, visit her blog at www.pamgarrison.typepad.com.

She remembers

Pam remembers growing up with a mother who sewed, oil painted, and crafted. Her father also always created and built many things. A few years ago, when Pam found herself in charge of props for her kids' school play, her dad learned to weld and made a birdcage big enough for a child to go in and out of. Pam also remembers her aunt Bonnie, a very talented artist. "One big memory of my childhood is being at my aunt Bonnie's home and seeing her craft building (which was actually a little shed). I admired her art studio and the world of artistic possibilities it held … and that it was all hers!"

Laurie Mika

Laurie Mika has become an iconic artist within the polymer clay community as she composes what she calls "mixed-media mosaics" with clay tiles that tell rich and compelling narratives. When she is not traveling the world to teach her techniques, she enjoys her home and studio in sunny southern California.

DETAILS & INTRICACIES

Illuminated manuscripts and gold-gilded devotional panels from Medieval and early Renaissance art are at the top of the list of things that inspire Laurie Mika. Museums like the Getty in Los Angeles are where Laurie treks to in order to view such objects up close and personal. "I also love antique medieval reliquaries, especially the little ones that are pure silver or gold and embedded with jewels," says Laurie. "They are often miniature architectural masterpieces that look like houses or churches. The fact that they hold relics is icing on the inspiration cake." Laurie also loves going into churches and gothic cathedrals, where she can find the kind of magnificence that she seeks — often found in the architectural details and stained glass art contained within.

Jewelry is another big source of inspiration for Laurie. "I love the work of many of the Israeli beaded jewelry artists like Ayala Bar," she says. "The intricacies of their designs amaze and inspire me, and I look for ways to incorporate that sensibility into my own work."

The other main source of inspiration for Laurie is rubber stamps — of which she has a large and always growing collection. "There are some that are just incredible and I can't wait to try them out in my work and to put my own spin on someone else's designs," says Laurie.

AND THEN THERE WAS LIGHT

Laurie's collection of rubber stamps is housed in her grandmother's antique sideboard — one of her storage units in her 300-square-foot studio that was built as an addition to her home. "The addition was built specifically to be a studio so it was nice to design some of the features in it like a small sink area for cleaning my brushes," says Laurie. "We also went through quite a bit of structural engineering drama to get permits to pour concrete floors up on the second floor of our home. I am so glad we pursued this … because even if I spill stuff on the floors, it looks great!"

Large windows that let the sunlight in throughout the day were also part of the design. "It feels like a perch in the front of the house where I am able to see down the street and keep tabs on what's happening outside," says Laurie. "It is nice not to feel isolated from my neighborhood or from the rest of my house. I feel very fortunate to 'go to work' without leaving home."

Sturdy metal drawers that are typically used to store tools in the garage are one of Laurie's favorite organizational units for the studio. She uses them to house her many small components that are incorporated into her mixed-media mosaics.

Saint Francis of Assisi

This deep sense of gratitude for the studio that Laurie has today is largely due to past struggles of having to carve out smaller and darker spaces in order to create. "In the old days, up until about 12 years ago, my studio consisted of a small portable drafting table," explains Laurie. "It moved from room to room in my house, often sharing bedrooms with one of our four kids. At one point, we actually had a secret little passageway through a closet in the master bedroom to an attic space in the rafters of the garage that was just large enough for my drafting table, my cart, and a light. I spent many hours working in there under the dim light."

She stays inspired

Books and magazines are what Laurie thumbs through when she is in a creative rut. She also peruses artistic Web sites and blogs, and cranks up some of her favorite tunes like Coldplay, Snow Patrol, and Dashboard Confessional. "I have recently found out about Pandora and I love it because I have created my own radio stations that play all of the music I love without commercials," says Laurie.

Her tip for organization & exercise to fuel creativity

TIP: Laurie recommends occasionally inviting company over to visit, which is one of the biggest motivators to do a thorough cleaning and organizing of one's studio space.

Exercise: Jot down some of your favorite words on separate pieces of scrap paper and place them in a jar. Without looking, select one of the paper scraps and a rubber stamp. Let the word and the stamp inspire a new art creation.

POLYMER CLAY ICON

As she basks in the light and space afforded to her in her current studio, Laurie works with her main artistic medium of polymer clay — for which she has become an icon. "I started by making polymer clay buttons, which evolved into tiles, and that led to the style of mixed-media mosaics that I currently make," says Laurie. "The mosaics are comprised of polymer clay tiles that have either been rubber stamped or painted, or both. I combine a variety of mixed-media materials into my mosaics. I mix the clay tiles with commercial tile, jewelry parts, beads, charms, buttons, and found objects."

In addition to the rich colors of her work, Laurie is interested in the deep and robust narrative quality that her art can achieve — which she attributes largely to her ability to fashion her own tiles by stamping into the clay to add words, sentences, and quotes.

CRAFTING NARRATIVES

The detailed beauty that can be seen on the surface of her works is what she hopes will draw an audience toward her work. But she hopes that that first look will eventually cause viewers to see what is at a deeper level. "That superficial first look is about seeing the decorative beauty of a richly embellished surface," says Laurie. "However, after that initial look, I hope the viewer is compelled to look deeper into the narrative content (and often overt messages) which are imbued in each piece.

"These messages have personal significance to me but it is my hope that the viewer will connect with my work using the experiences of their own lives to find meaning in what they are seeing. I have found that people really respond to the universality of the language of mosaics."

Her colors

PURPLE • GOLD • ORANGE • TURQUOISE

The bold and beautiful jewel tones of purple, gold, orange, and turquoise are what make up Laurie's color palette. "I like using this palette because all of the colors can be juxtaposed or mixed and they still work," explains Laurie. "They complement each other yet are singularly vibrant and alive and cast a 'reflective' quality."

She remembers

Laurie remembers sitting around in 6th grade drawing horses. "I was and still am a compulsive doodler," she says. "I also remember enjoying the craft-type presents that I would receive for gifts … like a beading set, perfume-making kit, and painting-by-number sets." In 7th grade, Laurie took her first art class with Mrs. Wright. "She was an enthusiastic teacher and she did a good job at nudging and nurturing her students," says Laurie.

Laurie Mika is a mixed-media artist who lives in southern California. She is the author of Mixed-Media Mosaics *(North Light, 2007). To learn more, visit* www.mikaarts.com.

Susan Tuttle

Susan Tuttle embraces all of life — the good, the bad, the happy, and the sorrowful. And through this embrace, she creates mixed-media and digital works of art that stir the soul and cause viewers to discover that there is art to be found in all facets of life.

HOPE & OPTIMISM

Susan Tuttle has always been inspired by people who shine and succeed in the face of adversity. "Hope and beauty can be found even in the darkest of places," says Susan. "I myself have had powerful experiences like this, where I have hit rock bottom, only to look up and see the light." Exploring how one rises up from the depths of despair is something Susan enjoys doing in her art — especially her digital art. "I am not afraid to go to the dark, hard places and explore them in my work," she says. But the great thing about exploring the dark is that light always follows, which is the case with Susan's work … where hope and optimism have a clear and strong presence in almost everything she creates.

Susan likes to find framed mirrors at thrift stores or garage sales. Once home, she paints the frames in colors that coordinate with her studio.

As a flutist and music educator, it is not surprising to learn that another huge source of inspiration for Susan is music. "Music is deeply rooted in my heart and I have always responded to it emotionally."

One of her favorite pieces is Symphony No. 3 by Henryk Gorecki (with soprano vocalist Dawn Upshaw). "When I wish to listen to this piece, I actually have to set some time aside for the experience — it gets me so emotionally charged and almost 'out of body,' so I need some recovery time afterwards," she says.

Susan views music as the strong force that guides her as she creates her art. This is especially true when she is creating digital art, where she is "plugged in" with her playlist ringing through her headset as she escapes into a universe that is all her own, to create in response to what she is hearing. "Sometimes I find myself creating depictions of the stories told in the songs," explains Susan. "The music often gives me the impetus I need to push my art into a deeper level."

Plain jars become extra special when the lids are adorned and embellished with fabric scraps and assorted bits and bobs.

Her colors

PALE PASTELS • CREAM • WHITE • BROWN

Susan's color palette changes from project to project. However, when she is working on her lighter, more whimsical works, she aims for pastels like pale pinks, aquamarine blues, lavender, light yellow, mint, cream, white, and brown. "This palette evokes a soft, innocent, playful, fun mood — appropriate for the nature of the pieces at hand," says Susan.

FUNCTION & STYLE

Though she describes her studio space as "tiny," she also describes it as "all mine." As a wife and mother of small children, having a space — regardless of the small size — is very important. The space allows Susan to turn down the volume of life's demands and summon the focus she needs to do what she is meant to do … what she is destined to do.

This studio was actually designed by Susan's husband, Howie, several years ago. When it was originally constructed, it yielded a space that was high in functionality but low in personality. "Actually, it had no personality," says Susan. "It functioned, but was devoid of style. And that bothered me."

So eventually, Susan embarked on a complete overhaul to make it uniquely hers, to draw out the artist within her soul. It is now a space with bright white walls, lots of vintage sheet music, and colorful countertops. Shelves with vintage tins, boxes, and suitcases also abound. And they house an endless array of fabrics, buttons, millinery flowers, and other knickknacks that all exude her personality.

LARGE & MINISCULE

Speaking of personality, Susan jokes that she has a "split personality" when it comes to expressing herself through art. "Thus you will find dirty, grungy gothic themes in my artwork and studio décor that pop up in between the girly pinks, aquamarine blues, and cupcakes," she says. Susan's personality is also split in terms of the scale that she tackles, which includes abstract intuitive paintings on large canvases, as well as tiny dollhouse miniatures.

All joking aside, Susan seems to tackle the large and the miniscule, the girlie and the macabre, because … well … she's curious. And she is able. Her artwork takes many forms — from mixed-media collage paintings to assemblage pieces, altered art to visual journaling, digital photography to artful blogging, and so much more.

The actions involved with her blog — poetically capturing photos with words — caused Susan to seek ways to elevate such actions as much as possible. "I felt a desire to learn computer programming in order to beautify my blog and create the design for my own Web site," she says. "I did just that and out blossomed my passions for graphic design and digital art. With my digital art, I am able to meld my love of creating mixed-media art with digital manipulations that I carry out in Photoshop."

Not only does Susan like to play and listen to music, she also enjoys incorporating sheet music as a collage element into many of her art designs.

JOYS & SORROWS

Given that Susan derives inspiration from those who can rise up from adversity, she accepts the fact that adversity must be part of life. And in her own life, there have been plenty of adverse situations, including a major car accident in her 20s and multiple miscarriages with her beloved Howie, prior to their ultimately welcoming a son and daughter into the world. "I believe that life's greatest lessons often come from adverse experiences and that incredible joy can be born from pain," says Susan.

She stays inspired

When Susan's creative well runs dry, one of the things she loves to do is watch foreign and independent films. "I am inspired by the 'off the beaten path' storylines and unique cinematography that often accompanies these types of films," says Susan. "I like to watch movies that take me to places that are very different from my experience here in Maine. They open up my eyes to new possibilities for living, and thus for making art."

She remembers

In preschool, Susan and her classmates made their first footprint paintings. "We were required to step into a pan filled with paint and then walk around on a large sheet of paper," she says. "That definitely made a strong impression on me … who knows, maybe it was the beginning of my interest in large-scale abstract painting."

"During times of adversity, Howie and I have always been determined to find the lessons to be learned instead of allowing ourselves to be swallowed up by our anger and grief. We learned that we could hold both joy and sorrow at the same time."

That she is able to embrace both the joys and sorrows of life is reflected in her art. "I believe my artwork comes from a place that is more than me," she says. "Art is tethered to something much greater that is meant to flow through me to others."

Susan Tuttle is a mixed-media artist who resides in the mid-coast region of Maine with her husband and two young children. She is author of Exhibition 36: Mixed-Media Demonstrations and Explorations (North Light, 2009). Her second book will focus on technique-based digital art. Susan is a frequent contributor to Stampington & Company publications and a variety of other mixed-media art books. To learn more, visit her Web site at www.ilkasattic.com and her blog at www.ilkasattic. blogspot.com.

By painting elements from nature — like twigs, branches, and driftwood — Susan is able to infuse a mood of innocence and playfulness into her compositions.

AUTHENTICITY & SPIRIT

There are two main sources of inspiration for Ulla: authenticity and spirit. For Ulla, authenticity is found when using findings from the past to create newly imagined objects with complete sincerity. It is found when one toils at her craft by searching for design solutions with whatever medium is being used — be it paperclay, textiles, or even shrink plastic. It's about being real and being part of a community of like-minded people who seek no shortcuts to crafting beauty. "I feel so lucky to live in a wonderful neighborhood filled with creative women," she says. "There are at least half a dozen working women artists within a block of our house. Walking across the street or around the corner to ask for advice, have lunch, or just 'chill' is a daily occurrence for all of us."

The spirit that Ulla names as her second source of inspiration belongs to the "other world" reality of fairy tales, folk tales, and gothic whimsy. "I am not particularly religious but am moved deeply by religious art," she explains. "I try to keep a sunny disposition but find inspiration in the dark, gothic, and macabre. I adore tales that transport you to a different time and place. I am a true romantic at heart."

Ulla Milbrath

Ulla Milbrath adores teaching and sharing her knowledge about creating art to students willing to learn. This teaching takes place regularly at a wondrous storefront in Berkeley, California, called Castle in the Air. Ulla's lessons also can be found on her wildly popular blog (*www.ullam.typepad.com*) where she shares generously with her faithful readers.

Birdcages aren't just for birds. Ulla actually likes to use birdcages in her studio to house votive candles. When the candles become lit, they cast a most beautiful illumination through the wires.

A SLICE OF HEAVEN

During college, Ulla always turned her one-bedroom apartments into areas where every square foot would function as her studio space. "I would eat, drink, and sleep art," she says. After college, Ulla and her husband rented two-bedroom apartments or homes and always had one of the rooms dedicated as Ulla's studio. "At one point, I had three employees plus myself working in a tiny bedroom all at the same time," says Ulla. "It wasn't until we bought our first home that I finally was able to get a studio outside the house, with space to move around.

"We bought our current home mainly because it has a double garage that extends into the backyard — the perfect space for my studio. My husband walled off the back half and put in a new floor, windows, a skylight, and French doors. The doors open up onto a lovely little deck with an old apple tree on one side and a romantic rose garden and labyrinth on the other. For me it is pure heaven. I can walk away from the house to 'work,' and close the door at night when I come home."

Ulla embraces the challenge of mixing many mediums together in her art projects. Paper, glitter, fabrics, clay, and elements from nature are layered to yield magnificently unexpected creations.

82

Her colors

ANTIQUE WILDFLOWER GARDEN

Ulla adores the faded colors of old 18th-century tapestries and embroideries, as well as the sparks of color that wildflowers give in early spring. She describes this palette as "antique wildflower garden." Says Ulla: "There is something romantic and soothing about this palette that speaks of yesterdays and happy memories but also points to wonderful tomorrows."

CASTLE COMMUNITY

After receiving her degree in textile design and wearable art, Ulla spent 10 years making jewelry and one-of-a-kind art dolls and selling her dolls at fairs across California. In the late 1990s, Ulla taught high school art, specializing in ceramics and beginning art skills. In 2003 when schools were making up budget shortfalls by cutting arts curriculums, Ulla found herself in search of a new path that would allow her to continue with her passion for art. "Almost by accident I found a new job teaching crafts to adults at a wonderful shop in Berkeley called Castle in the Air," she says (*www.castleintheair.biz*). "Here I was given free reign as to what I wanted to teach, as long as my projects kept an emphasis on paper and paper goods."

Since 2003, Ulla has worked at Castle in the Air and taught a variety of art classes including paper theaters, altered books, soldered jewelry and reliquaries, paperclay sculpting, and many other paper-related art forms. In addition to teaching classes, Ulla has created window displays and products to sell for the shop. "I feel like I am part of a family here at the Castle, and we share many ideas and projects freely," she says.

When not working at Castle in the Air, Ulla juggles assorted projects using textiles, and most recently a new endeavor of painting on porcelain. "I find it very difficult to limit myself when it comes to mediums," says Ulla. And one of the most important mediums for her has become the computer, which she uses to manage her blog that welcomes more than 2,500 visitors a day.

Because Ulla teaches many classes on paper theaters and altered books, she dedicates a large chunk of her studio space to store her collection of books that can be used as samples and class supplies.

She stays inspired

When Ulla faces a creative rut, she changes her routine. "Sometimes I will take a day and go to the city to just look around, visit my favorite shops, or stay with a friend," she says. "I love to go antiquing. Spending a few hours updating my 'idea books' or ripping magazines also helps."

OTHERWORLDLY ADVENTURES

When she considers what might lie in front of her, Ulla definitely sees teaching as part of her future, as nothing gives her more pleasure than sharing with others what she knows or has discovered while creating art. "I adore teaching and learn so much in return from my students," she says.

But given her adventuresome spirit and her love of nature, it's not surprising to learn that Ulla would also love to try her hand at welding large outdoor sculptures or even a garden gate someday … perhaps some prancing deer or flying owls welded in steel across the garage. "Doing something large with a dangerous tool like a torch seems otherworldly to me right now, but intriguing nevertheless," she says.

Ulla Milbrath is a multi-media artist who lives in northern California. To learn more about her art and life, visit www.ullam.typepad.com.

She remembers

The earliest memory of creativity that Ulla has is watching her mother hand paint and batik clothing. "When I was an infant she made one-of-a-kind wearable art and sold it in the streets of Sausalito," she says. "As a European immigrant, she was a sophisticated flower child. I still have skirts and dresses that we made together at that time, with my painting or appliqué and her sewing. She was my idol."

HEARTFELT FLAWS

For Suzie Millions, perfection is overrated. And though she is not formally trained, Suzie delights in her self-taught ability to collect items that are a little "off" or flawed and transform them into something marvelous. "For me, the flaws tell stories and convey a sense of humanity," she says.

"I'm inspired by heartfelt, handmade objects that reflect a sense of humanity ... wood hobby-craft shelves, matchstick, and Popsicle stick constructions, thrift store paintings, hand-painted plaster castings, hand-built ceramic objects, household cast-offs like bottles and jars, and other things of that sort."

Over the years of collecting such items that tug at her heart, Suzie's living space has transformed into an inspiration shrine of sorts. "We don't have room for a sofa in the cabin but we do have a comfy chair, and sometimes when I'm looking for inspiration, I settle into it and pay close scrutiny to these collected objects that I live with every day," she says. "Sometimes I get ideas for a direction to take in my own art, and sometimes the pieces themselves end up being part of my work."

Suzie Millions

Suzie Millions is passionate about gathering "discards" from the past to create new art items that evoke a sense of history and meaning. She is author of *The Complete Book of Retro Crafts* (Lark, 2008) and lives in an old cabin in western North Carolina with her best friend Lance. She seeks to create works that become portals to the past.

So passionate is Suzie about all things retro that she not only creates retro-style art, she also lives with retro-style décor. From a lamp made of a trophy base to Felix the Cat mugs and more, every facet of Suzie's world exudes her style and passion.

Matchboxes, plastic strawberry cartons, and other everyday "discards" are what Suzie frequently uses to upcycle into totally hip and totally unconventional art.

She stays inspired

Fueling momentum is the key to combating ruts for Suzie. "I'm far less likely to get into a creative rut if I'm able to maintain a bit of momentum," she says. "Keeping a creative thread going, even if it's just accumulating research, giving thought to projects, or jotting occasional notes, helps keep momentum going and staves off potential ruts."

UNCONVENTIONAL CHIC

"Conventional" is not a word that describes Suzie's art studio. Not now, not ever. Currently, her space is within an industrial loft space that Suzie describes as "a little bit Grandpa Munster's basement lab and a little bit Pee Wee's playhouse." Most of the cabinets, storage containers, and other fixtures are from thrift stores or yard sales, while other things are "discards" found from unassuming curbs. "I spend entirely too much time and energy acquiring things other people deem unfit to keep in their homes," says Suzie.

And once Suzie gathers all of her findings in her studio, she likes to use all such items for something other than their intended purpose. "An old toy airport serves as my desk organizer," says Suzie. "A decoupaged wood cookie jar holds supply receipts, vintage suitcases and canisters are great storage containers, a toy refrigerator holds a few favorite tsatskes, and a tiered dessert server keeps studio essentials handy."

Prior to her current studio space, Suzie has been known to have her kitchens serve double duty as a place to store and prepare food, and a place to store and prepare art. Not surprisingly, Suzie's son grew up finding it perfectly normal to have cans of soup and bags of rice regularly juxtaposed against bags of cement and jars of aquarium gravel.

Aside from her kitchen/studio experiences, Suzie names one of her all-time favorite work spaces to be a 29-foot Airstream trailer. "A friend needed a place to store it for a few years so I traded free storage for permission to use it as a studio," she says. "I was happy for my friend when he was finally ready to embark on his cross-country adventure, but sad to see my super-swell silver studio hitched to the back of his pick-up and headed down the driveway."

WHERE EVERYONE BELONGS

When Suzie's son, Andrew, was just about 4 years old, he offered a description of her creations by saying that "My mom likes to put things on other things where they don't belong." This description has become Suzie's favorite way of describing what she does.

"I make memory jars, shrines, dioramas, shard art, linoleum prints, reverse paintings on glass, and multi-media assemblages," says Suzie. "Much of my multi-media work includes vintage linens, dishes, ephemera, and domed glass."

Much of Suzie's work has been music-related — early American blues, soul, and rock — but over the years, her focus has broadened to include the culture that gave birth to and nurtured that music. "In my art, I strive to make things that emanate a sense of history," she says. "I repurpose materials gathered from the junk world."

Her colors

CHARTREUSE GREEN • DEEP FOREST GREEN
CHOCOLATE BROWN • CARAMEL

Although Suzie adjusts her color palette from project to project, the colors that she gravitates toward time and time again are chartreuse green, deep forest green, chocolate brown, and caramel. "This palette evokes the mood of the early 1950s for me," says Suzie.

She remembers

Suzie remembers growing up within a highly creative family. "My mother and sisters were all artistic," she says. "My aunt Lucy drew fashion ads for the local newspaper, my aunt Chris did 'Chalk Talks' in church and my mom made all kinds of things, including construction paper holiday cutouts that in my dreams I will find someday on a junking junket."

But the one person who really spurred Suzie's artistic ambitions was her older sister, Connie. "I grew up trying very hard to be as creative as she was," says Suzie. "She made up art projects for herself while still in elementary and middle school. Inspired by a TV series, she wrote dossiers on 3" x 5" cards and glued faces clipped from the Sears® catalog to them to make a file of "spy identities" to choose from when we played in the backyard."

When sources for inspiration become exhausted indoors, Suzie enjoys stepping outside to enjoy the beauty of nature that is found in her front yard and backyard.

PORTALS TO CREATIVITY

From the materials to the color palette to the aesthetics of her designs, Suzie makes a deliberate effort, "like zigzagging on the sidewalk to avoid stepping on cracks," to make artistic choices that allow the piece to relate to the historical era that it is rooted in.

"I would like to provide people a glimpse through a dusty window into a moment in time" she says. "I would like them to feel that they have been transported into that other era, and then brought back, enriched by the experience. I think that's why I like using images behind glass, frequently domed glass, because it requires the viewer to actually engage with the piece and peer in.

"It's great to have a designated studio space, and it definitely helps with productivity, but that doesn't mean that you have to confine your creative aesthetic to your studio and your art. Let it spill into your yard, your parties, the way you dress, the way you present meals. Each of us is the result of our own unique life experiences. Share it. Live your art."

Suzie Millions is author of The Complete Book of Retro Crafts *(Lark, 2008). To learn more about her art, visit* www.suziemillions.com.

Her tips for organization & exercises to fuel creativity

TIP: Because Suzie uses a lot of repurposed materials in her work, she is constantly bringing into her studio an odd assortment of stuff from all kinds of places. "I keep an incoming bin where I can drop these things into until I can take the time to put them in their place," she says. "By maintaining one designated incoming spot, my space stays neater, and I can focus on what I came to the studio to work on while I'm still brimming with fresh ideas and eager to get to work."

Exercise: If you're right-handed, try creating with your left hand, and vice versa. Even if it's for just a doodle, you'll be surprised to see art that can be created by either hand.

TIP: Suzie stores materials according to what they are made of, and not what their intended use is. "To find something, all I have to do is ask myself, 'What is it made of?' to quickly lead me to what I need," she says.

Exercise: Ask a child to create something with a supply you have on hand. Examine how the child uses the supply, and learn a different way of using the material.

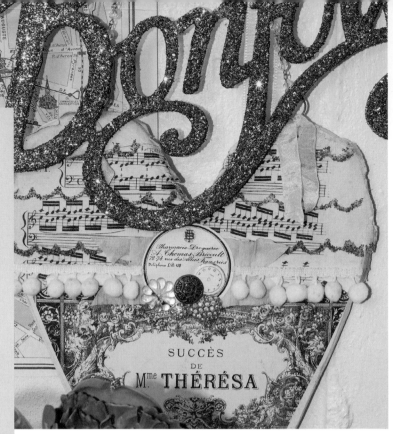

Teresa McFayden

Teresa McFayden is a mixed-media artist who is passionate about creating objects of beauty. She is also founder of Silver Bella — an annual art retreat that inspires and equips women from all walks of life to be creative.

EXTREME SENSATIONS

Teresa believes that in order to know joy, one needs to know pain. And it's reflecting on the extreme instances of both sensations from her past that serve as the greatest source of inspiration for her art. "Extreme pain and extreme joy … they are sensations that are so tragic or so beautiful that you want to express them to either get rid of them if they are painful, or to share them if they are joyful," she says.

Unconditional love from family members and significant votes of confidence from college professors are some experiences that Teresa sites as examples of joyful inspiration. In terms of pain, it is of course different from person to person, but Teresa views that even the negative can inspire artwork that doesn't necessarily exude an aesthetic of "pretty and happy," but is valid nonetheless and deserving of inspired expression.

The other main source of inspiration that Teresa names is the power and strength that she gains from her deep faith. "Often times, I feel like I work in unison with The Holy Spirit," she says. "It's very powerful."

In her basement-turned-studio, Teresa houses a large circular dinner table where she loves to spread out and create. The smaller rectangular desk is where she keeps her business-related tasks organized.

ECLECTIC WORK-IN-PROGRESS

"My studio is many places and has many shapes and sizes," says Teresa. "If you think of a studio as a creative space just for you, then I would have to confess that there are many studios that my thoughts and creative process call home … sometimes my car, or my laptop, a journal, my office, or even a corner seat at the library."

But the larger day-to-day studio space that Teresa describes as a "continual work-in-progress" is the one in the basement of her home. "It's a studio that I see as a very large canvas, and one that I enjoy re-creating a couple of times a year," she says. The walls of her basement studio are made of cinderblocks and the concrete floor is covered with off-white shag area rugs. The shag rugs have been newly paired with pink champagne velvet swags that nicely cover up the shelves in which Teresa stores many of her supplies. "It's taken on a 'vintage shab' look, yet is still pretty eclectic in spirit," says Teresa. "This is the largest space I've ever had and I don't see it getting much larger than it is now."

Though Teresa takes advantage of the many places in her world that she can claim as her creative space at any given moment, she appreciates being able to have the basement studio as all her own. Says Teresa: "Over time, you accumulate things and need a place to put them … but mostly over time you yearn for a place to step out of the everyday world and into your own personal space … a place you can turn down everything else in your daily life and turn up the creative energy that waits patiently for its chance to sing."

Her colors

BLACK • CREAM

Though at times Teresa gravitates toward other colors, she never tires of black and cream. "They are classic mainstays for me, which evoke a sense of earthiness and calmness," she says.

FREEDOM TO CREATE

As a mixed-media artist, Teresa delights in the freedom to create a huge variety of art with many different types of mediums including paper, fabric, metal, sewing machines, scissors, needles, thread, paint, charcoal, and quite possibly every kind of glue that exists. "I tend to get bored using the same medium all of the time, so I give myself lots of mediums to create with," she says.

Teresa is not only passionate about creating art objects, but she is also passionate about creating opportunities where women can feel connected, empowered, and inspired. This passion is what led her in 2005 to found Silver Bella — an art retreat that takes place every winter in Omaha, Nebraska, where talented artists convene to teach attendees unique art projects. Aside from the art projects, Teresa tends to every detail of the retreat experience so each attendee feels pampered and special. The first year, Silver Bella drew a crowd of 75 participants. Now, it is a much sought-out event that draws nearly 200 attendees. "I love to try and outdo myself each year," says Teresa. "Just when I think it's not possible, I find a way … maybe not in one facet of the event, but in another. It's a fun personal challenge."

Her tips for organization & exercises to fuel creativity

TIP: For Teresa, a big desk frees one's mind to really spread out. "My desk is actually a kitchen table that seats six people," she says.

Exercise: See what you can create when your supplies are limited. For example, gather five collage elements into a small basket and see what you can compose, without reaching for additional supplies.

TIP: Teresa believes that because artists are such visual people, it's important to keep supplies in open or see-through containers. She is also a big fan of trays, which she uses to gather supplies from her assorted containers in order to carry the items back and forth from her desk.

Exercise: After you read a good book or see a great performance, create a project that could symbolize a character from the story.

She stays inspired

At any given time, Teresa is swimming in the many deadlines that she juggles for magazines, books, zines, and other special projects. And as much as deadlines take a toll on her, she believes that having deadlines is one of the biggest ways to get out of creative ruts.

Vintage player piano rolls make the perfect window treatment in Teresa's studio, as light beautifully casts through the teeny, tiny holes of the pale and timeworn rolls of paper.

She remembers

Some of Teresa's earliest memories of creativity is being with her grandmother on her farm and playing with clay. "Her gentle spirit made for a fine teacher," she remembers. Teresa also remembers a group of free-spirited high school girls who invited her and other neighboring children to create at the picnic table the park. "During the summer months, we'd gat create whatever they taught us — like stringing shell necklaces, painting 'Love is' wall plaques, and stamping with potatoes."

TUGS AT THE HEARTSTRINGS

Whether it's her one-of-a-kind pieces, customized kits made available through her beautiful blog, or her beloved Silver Bella event, Teresa's hope is that her audience is able to gain happiness, tranquility, and sometimes humor from what she has to offer. She also hopes that at times, what she does will tug at people's heartstrings … and perhaps inspire them to reflect on the extreme joys of the past.

Teresa McFayden is a mixed-media artist who lives in Omaha, Nebraska. To learn more, visit www.teresamcfayden.typepad.com.

PLACE·TO·BE·TRUE. A·PLACE·TO·BE·YOU:

DRAWN TO COLOR

Ever since she was little, Joanna Figueroa has been intrigued and inspired by color. Today, color is at the heart of all that she creates — both in her artwork and her business. "Color inspires me. Patterns and designs are necessary and beautiful and are vehicles to help communicate … but color is what draws me in," says Joanna. "Of course vintage color palettes are what I work with but color of any kind is what I always see first — whether I hate something or love it."

Whether she's taking a drive in the country, visiting a stationery store, shopping at a favorite retailer, taking a walk on the beach, or tending to plants in the garden, it's color that inspires her to truly see all that is around her. "There is something that physically draws me to certain vintage color palettes … especially those that I find in vintage book illustrations and French advertising posters and products," adds Joanna.

Joanna Figueroa

Joanna Figueroa is a master at deploying her imagination and fortitude to create something from nothing. She is also a master at creating feelings with unique color combinations. She uses her skills as proprietor of Fig Tree & Co. to create quilts and fabric designs that make a colorful impact on the quilting and sewing community.

DRAWING THE LINE

Like many artists who juggle the demands of raising children and keeping a home, Joanna has had to "make do" for many years, in terms of her creative space. "I think my favorite was when my second son was born, we divided one bedroom in half — one half for the studio and the other half for the nursery," recalls Joanna. "So one side of the room consisted of a crib, changing table, and a rocking chair … and the other side had two bookshelves jammed full of fabric and a studio desk piled high with fabric, books, and a sewing machine. You could literally have drawn a line straight down the middle of the room."

The studio that Joanna currently enjoys is made up of two separate rooms, which is the entire second floor that was added to her 1930s Tudor-style home. "It is a light, airy, warm space — one side for the fabric part of my job and an attached office for the computer and design portion of the business," she says. "The fabric studio is easily my favorite room."

A custom-built quilt rack is positioned against one of the walls of Joanna's studio. She uses it to hang quilts, as well as small fabric swatches and quilt blocks in progress.

ECLECTIC ART

It took Joanna a long time to consider herself an artist. She saw herself as a crafter, doodler, and creative person … someone who enjoyed working with her hands. But it took her a long time before she allowed herself to claim the title of "artist." Says Joanna: "I fell into that trap of believing that artists had to be formally trained and work with a traditional or fine art types of mediums. The fact that I had been assembling color palettes and looking for prints that worked together since I was 8 years old, somehow didn't really qualify for me when I looked at the definition of 'artist' as an adult."

Today, Joanna refers to herself as an "eclectic artist." It's a term that reflects what she does on a regular basis, which is working with fabrics to create quilts and other related products. "Fabric is definitely my favorite medium of all the ones I have worked with and it seems that I have dabbled in many mediums over the years … like inks, pastels, paper making, print making, pottery, collage, and jewelry," says Joanna.

Her tips for organization & exercises to fuel creativity

TIP: For Joanna, a good filing system is a must for staying organized. "You have to be able to find what you need and you don't want to waste precious time," she says.

Exercise: Find a greeting card with an illustration that you like. Gather fabrics with colors from the greeting card and re-create the look and feel of the illustration with your fabric "palette."

TIP: After the flurry of rallying a project to its completion, Joanna insists on cleaning up. "Cleaning up between projects clears my mind and helps me transition to the next project," she says.

Exercise: Visit an antique store to find a vintage quilt or quilt remnant. Use what you find to create something new — like a pillow, a wall hanging, a pincushion, or a sewing machine cover.

For Joanna, the beauty of quilting is that it is an art form that yields objects that are artistic and utilitarian. She likes that the act of snuggling up in a comfy chair can be done with great style, in the presence of quilts.

"Since I have focused on fabric projects and fabric design, I have worked primarily with colored pencils, gouache, and computer design. Most of my fabric collections include any number of sources from vintage fabrics, and hand sketches to little painted roughs and computer design. I almost never just stick to one source or one medium. It is kind of a random process when I really think about it. I never know exactly where I will end up when I start."

RESILIENCE & RISK

Aside from her passion for color, Joanna wonders whether her experience of immigrating to the United States from Poland at the tender age of 7 may have contributed to the success she enjoys as proprietor of Fig Tree & Co. — a business that has produced 15 fabric lines for MODA, self-published more than 100 quilt and sewing patterns, and collaborated on many other products.

"Starting life over here in the United States as a small girl without any extended family, without knowing a word of English … it was a tough way to grow up but it surely made me resilient," recalls Joanna.

"I was not afraid of risk and was able to see possibilities when others couldn't. I doubt that I would have decided to start my own company had I not watched my dad build one when we came to this country."

Her colors

**APPLE GREENS • TANGERINES
PLUMS • CHOCOLATE BROWNS
AQUA BLUES • TOMATO REDS
SEA FOAM GREENS**

Colors found in vintage books are what resonate with Joanna. So passionate is she about this palette that she has trademarked a line of products utilizing the colors as Fresh Vintage™. "The colors connect to our desire to create a home and be current at the same time," says Joanna.

Joanna Figueroa is a fabric designer and quilter who lives in the San Francisco Bay Area with her husband and children. She is proprietor of Fig Tree & Co. To learn more, visit her Web site at www.figtreequilts.com or her blog at www.figtreequilts.typepad.com.

Alisa Burke

Alisa Burke rocks the canvas by painting stretches of it with her audacious strokes of bold colors. The canvas is then cut and upcycled into highly desired items like handbags, wall hangings, and jewelry. Alisa creates her fresh, urban aesthetic as a mixed-media artist in sunny San Diego, California.

INDEPENDENCE THROUGH ART

For Alisa Burke, majoring in fine art at Portland State University is one of the most significant life occurrences that shaped her into who she has become. "It takes a lot of courage to declare painting and print making as your area of study because there is no job stability or guarantees when you decide to put money into an art education," says Alisa.

Though being a full-time artist has been her goal since her courageous decision to major in art, Alisa has — like so many artists — juggled assorted day jobs while pursuing her art career in order to make ends meet. Alisa finds her current day job as Assistant Director of Print and Brand Marketing at the University of San Diego to be quite interesting. However, she remains driven to eventually make a full-time living as an artist — without support from any other source.

Her organizational tip & exercise to fuel creativity

TIP: Given that her creative process is so expressive, Alisa doesn't believe in being that organized. "I let myself be messy and not worry about staying organized while creating," she explains.

Exercise: If you've learned rules about composition or color, try creating a piece where you deliberately break those rules. You may discover a new effect or technique in the process.

In fact, this drive for independence through art is what Alisa names as her greatest source of inspiration. "My greatest inspiration comes from wanting to be an artist full-time," says Alisa. "I have balanced a day job with my creative career for what seems like forever and the drive that I have comes from knowing one day that I will be able to work full-time as an artist." When days are long and challenging in her non-artistic reality, Alisa is most inspired and determined to work for another five or more hours into the night in her art studio.

Alisa drapes fabrics and treated canvas along a wall and edges of her desk to create areas where supplies can be stored out of sight.

GARAGE FOUND

The studio that Alisa speaks of is actually a converted garage in the first home that she and her husband, Andy, have purchased. "During our house hunting, we agreed that we needed a place with a garage that we would convert into my studio," says Alisa.

Prior to this converted garage studio, Alisa remembers feeling pretty confined in nooks and crannies she'd carve out for herself in previous apartments. More often than not, she'd find herself working on the kitchen floor. "I often prefer painting on the ground so I can crawl around my large surface," says Alisa. "When I lived in a tiny studio apartment, I created anywhere I could fit ... on the floor, countertops, even the bathtub!"

Her colors
RED • GREEN • BLACK

Alisa is most attracted to very bright and rich colors. "I have always used a lot of Cadmium Red in my artwork and I love pairing it with a cool green," says Alisa. "I always make use of black — lots of bold black lines, shapes, and marks." When using her favorite color palette, Alisa works with great speed and expression until the piece "just feels right."

PAINT, CUT, STITCH

Fans of Alisa's work would not be surprised to know that artistically speaking, Alisa could not live without paint, canvas, and a sewing machine. In her studio, Alisa works with bold paint colors to create designs on canvas that could be described as "urban," "street," and "contemporary." Neither her color palette nor her design aesthetic are for the faint of heart.

And while Alisa still paints pictures to hang on the wall and for gallery shows, much of what she creates currently are one-of-a-kind purses made from yards and yards of canvas that she paints and then cuts and sews. "I will often spend days painting raw unstretched canvas that is full of layers, color, texture, and images and then cut it up and sew with it," says Alisa.

Through these handbags and accessories, Alisa wants to evoke feelings in those who view her work, and to redefine traditional materials into unexpected objects. "We are so accustomed to looking at art as something to look at or hang on the wall but I think that everyday objects can be art," says Alisa.

She is inspired by …

- A great movie
- A passionate song
- A colorful skirt
- Color in the sky
- Time with like-minded friends
- Good food

EMULATING PASSION

Aside from the foundation of love, support, and freedom that Alisa's husband provides for her every day, Alisa credits her parents, Jon and Linda Burke, as the people who have inspired her most to pursue her passion for art. Jon and Linda are potters and in every house that Alisa and her parents lived, there was a huge studio space with potter's wheels, a kiln, glazes, and lots of tools.

"For as long as I can remember, I wanted to be an artist and my parents always encouraged and supported this aspiration and never once made me feel that it was silly or unattainable," says Alisa. "They lived a creative life even when there was little money at times … they took huge risks, were willing to embrace change … they are brave and creative people who I will always strive to emulate."

Alisa Burke is a mixed-media artist who lives in San Diego, California. She is the author of Canvas Remix *(North Light, 2008). To learn more about Alisa Burke, visit* www. alisaburke.com *or* www.alisaburke.blogspot.com.

STRETCHING IMAGINATION & RESOURCES

Imagining a time that was slower and more deliberate is what inspires Nicol Sayre. The kind of time when a mother, whose child wished for a store-bought doll, was challenged to create something from items on hand. Or perhaps a time when the dressmaker of old was challenged to create a ball gown for a discerning customer. "These are all artists of the past who didn't have the luxuries we have today — their challenges and dreams are a driving force in me," says Nicol. "I want to make and do everything myself and not rely on anything that can be bought, or is pre-made, or readily available in stores." In other words, Nicol is not interested in shortcuts or easy solutions. She wants to stretch herself, much like those from the past were forced to stretch resources and imaginations to create objects of beauty.

In order to leverage her penchant for the past, Nicol has made it her life's work to hunt for vintage treasures that she turns to when her creative muse awakens. And this hunt is what Nicol names as another huge source of inspiration. "I am so inspired by just opening my little drawers full of trinkets or sifting through antique fashion prints or surfing the Internet for vintage dressmaking techniques," she says.

As Nicol ponders magical stories from the past, she develops an insatiable desire to create new stories by refashioning vintage objects. "I want to create all the things that live inside my head," she says. "I lay awake at night and think of the mechanics of a piece I want to make, and I delve through my books on antique dolls or sift through my fabrics waiting for the right combination to emerge."

Nicol Sayre

Nicol is passionate about creating dolls that exude the beauty and artistry of a bygone era. Each doll is created entirely by Nicol's hands, and the dolls are collected by admirers who seek to keep alive the stories and spirit of the past.

Treasures from the past — like vintage photos and books, ceramic frozen Charlottes, and tattered dressforms — are what Nicol surrounds herself with as she channels stories from long-ago to inspire her art.

Wire baskets of all shapes, sizes, and colors abound in Nicol's studio. They allow her to store her favorite fabrics and trims in an orderly and visible fashion.

A FEELING OF HOME

Once upon a time, when Nicol didn't have a dedicated space to call her own, she used to paint and sculpt at the kitchen sink. "You never knew whether there would be doll heads or dinner in the oven," she laughs. "I had a tiny upstairs bedroom in which to sew and create that was constantly spilling over into the rest of the house. Luckily my family was so patient with me for over 20 years of creating with them right in the midst of it on a daily basis."

Today, the space in which Nicol creates is a second floor room that was completely remodeled and refashioned to transform into her studio. It is a space with lovely natural light and large windows with beautiful views of the garden, hills, and trees. The high ceilings, clean wood floors, and light-colored trims provide Nicol with a feeling of clarity that helps her create. "It is a little spot of my own with plenty of space to spread out and contain all of my supplies and collections," she says. "I love having a space for all of my trinkets and inspirations so no matter where I look, it is a feeling of home."

DOLLS WITH HISTORY

With papier mâché and collected elements from the past, Nicol creates dolls that are infused with a sense of history. "I hand sculpt and paint each one and give them the patina of another time," she says. "I am especially inspired by antique dolls like wooden milliners' models, old papier mâché French and English dolls, and china dolls."

In addition to creating the actual dolls, Nicol delights in costuming them. "I love the timeworn quality of antique fabrics and trims, and the dolls all gowned in the romantic styles of the past … with boned corsets, wire or wooden hoopskirts, tiny waists, and voluminous skirts," she says. "I love to adorn them with paper trinkets fashioned of antique ledgers and paper from antique books. They are crowned with bonnets of straw, velvets, millinery flowers, and flowing ribbons. I love old papers, fashion trinkets like pocketbooks and slippers, memory boxes from old ledger papers, little dolls, and found objects."

So admired are Nicol's dolls that over the years, the number of admirers who collect Nicol's works has steadily grown. And though there is a sense of mourning that Nicol experiences when each special creation leaves her for a new home, she knows that it is all a lovely process that helps stories of old to live on.

Her tip for organization & exercise to fuel creativity

TIP: If Nicol can't see it, she will forget it's there. This is why she recommends storing supplies in ways that make them visible. "I like to use flat enamel trays or wire baskets that are never too deep or things get buried," she says. "I use antique flat soup bowls stacked up with my buttons and metal findings. I stack my fabrics by color and by weight so I know just the stack to look for."

Exercise: Gather a piece of vintage fabric and divide it in two. Use one piece to create something in the morning and the other to create something in the evening. Examine how differently you create, depending on the time of day.

She stays inspired

Given the high demand for her dolls, Nicol rarely has time to make things for herself. So when she is in a creative rut, that's when she allows herself to work on a project just for herself. "I get out my old sketchbooks and revisit ideas I have had in the past," she says.

"I usually work in an all-or-nothing fashion. Days and nights for weeks before a show I am working like a mad person and then afterwards I have to take a couple of days to recharge and recover." After the recovery, jumping back into the swing of things takes huge effort. To make it happen, she exercises what she calls the "three-hour and three-day challenge," where she allows herself three hours to get into the work and three days of working non-stop, until all ideas are actualized.

ROOM FOR COMFORT

When Nicol started making dolls nearly 20 years ago, she never dreamed that she'd achieve such success. "The first time I ever did a show and so many people actually 'got' me and my dolls and understood what I was trying to convey to the world … that was such an incredibly enabling experience that I could show what was in my heart and soul, and they liked it!" she says.

The first national article about Nicol's dolls appeared in the September 2001 issue of *Home Companion*. And immediately after the issue hit newsstands, the 9/11 tragedy occurred. "I grieved with the rest of the world and doubted that anyone would want to buy dolls in the wake of such a tragedy," she says. "But after several days, the maelstrom hit. I was bombarded with requests for dolls. I realized then that no matter the tragedies of the world, there is always room and need for a little comfort and art for the soul."

Nicol Sayre is an artist who lovingly creates dolls that exude the spirit of a bygone era. To learn more, visit her Web site at www.nicolsayre.com or her blog at www.nicolsayre.typepad.com.

She remembers

Nicol's mother is a dressmaker, and Nicol fondly remembers her mother always staying up late at night, sewing for her customers. "Growing up, we did all kinds of crafts like sewing, needlework, and macramé," she says. "I made clothes for my dolls and bears, and drew fancy costumes with big hoopskirts and bows."

EXTRAORDINARY IDEAS

More than 30 years ago, Jo Packham found herself in the middle of Apple Arts — a store that she co-owned in Ogden, Utah, with her very best friend, Linda — and had a major "aha" moment. "I remember saying to Linda, 'You know what? We need to produce our own line of cross-stitch books,'" says Jo. From that day on, Jo would embark on a journey within the publishing world where she would found Chapelle, Ltd., a company that would align with major book publishers to produce more than 250 titles within the art and crafting field.

Not only did Jo create books on cross-stitching, but also books on quilting, painting, doll making, rubber stamping, knitting, and so much more. And in 2005, Jo worked with Sterling Publishing to create a book titled *Where Women Create* — one of Jo's best-selling books about extraordinary women and their creative spaces.

And speaking of extraordinary women, Jo points to Linda as one of the most extraordinary and supportive women she has ever known. "We have been friends since before junior high and she has always, always been there for me," says Jo. "She is kind, she is thoughtful, she is sincere, she is generous, she is compassionate, and she is everything that you need a friend to be."

Jo Packham

Jo Packham creates community, hope, and friendship through the beautiful publications she designs, including the new quarterly magazine based on her popular book, *Where Women Create*. She's been making her publishing magic happen at her headquarters in Ogden, Utah, where through the support of key people, Jo finds a way to tell the stories of some of the most extraordinary women of our time.

Having produced more than 250 of her own throughout her career, Jo has a special affinity for all sorts of books, and surrounds her studio with as many of them as she can. In different parts of her studio, books are stacked in piles large and small.

113

THE COUCH, THE ALCOVE & THE LOFT

Before she started her line of books, Jo's "studio" space was not larger than the couch that she sat on to stitch designs for her cross-stitch books. "Then I would move to the kitchen table to graph the patterns for printing," she explains. "It took a year or so until I bought myself a drafting table and put it in a spare bedroom so that the kitchen table could be used for eating and not for graphics. My studio stayed there until I became a single mom with two small children."

Eventually, Jo's operation blossomed into one where her partner designed the pieces and they hired staff to create the cross-stitch, so that Jo could be in charge of the business and public relations portion of the business. As she continued to experience success with her projects, she found herself in a three-story 1920s home, where on the second floor was a room for her office and on the third floor was an alcove that would become her creative space. "There in the alcove, I felt safe, happy, and most creative," says Jo. "But then life changes and we must make changes with it, so I sold the house and am now renting a loft-type apartment that has an unbelievable view of the city. My craft space is no longer my home but is part of my office on Historic 25th Street. For some, this is also a dream come true."

This space on Historic 25th has a first floor that houses Olive & Dahlia, which is a florist and garden store. The second floor is where all things related to *Where Women Create* happen, including the quarterly magazine that Jo worked in 2008 to launch in partnership with Stampington & Company. The demand for this magazine is so strong that it has become one of Stampington & Company's best-selling titles, where each issue to date has sold out. It is a magazine that has captured the imagination of creative women across the globe.

BITTER & SWEET SEASONS OF LIFE

As the studio space of Jo Packham has evolved, so too has her tempo as a person. A tempo influenced and inspired through her experiences of being a daughter, an entrepreneur, a mother, and best of all, a grandmother.

A few years ago, Jo's life tempo was dramatically impacted when her mother suffered a stroke. "All of a sudden I was aware of how precious and fragile life is and how little we can control it," says Jo. Eleven months after the stroke, Jo's mother passed away. "My mom had had more faith in me than I sometimes earned and she was the one who, in her quiet and steady wisdom, made me believe that I could truly do anything I wanted to do," says Jo. "She

Friends and family serve as the greatest source of inspiration for Jo. And the most special ones get front and center treatment, as Jo likes to frame and display photographs of her loved ones for the world to see.

had worked her way up to a good life from one that started in a tar paper shack with no running water as she crawled under the train to go to school. She was an inspiration and an example of hope and hard work."

With the sorrow that Jo endured with her mother's passing, one thing she knew for sure is that she would never again experience the same depth of sadness. "However, regardless of how much my heart ached, my mom continued to teach me that there wasn't anything that I couldn't do for myself or for someone who needed me," she says.

As this realization was crystallizing, Jo found herself, three days after her mother's stroke, meeting her twin grandchildren who were born to her beloved daughter, Sara, and Sara's husband. "The arrival of the twins proved yet again that life is fragile and precious and out of our control," says Jo. "They are both beautiful, wonderful children and I love them with all my heart. And being a Grammy is like nothing else in all the world … not that having my own children wasn't as important to me as my grandchildren, but when I had my children, I was young, ambitious, busy, and on a fast track. It's different for grandparents … maybe because we are older, wiser, slower, less ambitious … but those two little ones make me happier than anything else in the world."

Her tip for organization & exercise to fuel creativity

TIP: For Jo, the process of getting things organized is as much a creative pursuit as the process of making a project. "It is all about keeping things 'pretty' so that you enjoy looking at your boxes, you enjoy putting things away in them, and you enjoy just having them in your space," she says.

Exercise: Rather than keeping your photos in boxes or on your computer, print them out, place them in frames, and display them in your studio space. The next time you are in need of inspiration, gather your framed photos and other favorite treasures and rearrange them so that they are in some place new and unexpected. The creative reorganization will naturally lead you in a new and different direction for your next project.

DELIBERATE LEGACY OF HOPE

Older, wiser, steadier … and arguably much more deliberate is Jo Packham's life these days. It's a life that she doesn't take for granted because it took so much hard work to get to where she has come. The kind of hard work that her mother knew much about and would be applauding Jo for today. And regardless of the success Jo has experienced to date, she still finds herself combating fears and challenges found in everyday life to keep everything moving forward.

Through the books and magazines that she creates, Jo creates her art. And with it, a sense of community, hope, and friendship. Some would argue it's a legacy she has built. For Jo, it is a life of passion that she has led, fueled by the love and support of key people who have taught her that life is short, time is precious, and friendships, because they are rare, need to be treasured when found.

She remembers

Jo remembers always being surrounded by the creative energy of her mom. "She was very creative and patient enough to let me be creative," says Jo. "She taught me how to sew but my earliest creative memory is when I was in junior high school. I wanted to paint my room by myself and decorate it without any help.

"She told me I could and so I painted the walls chartreuse green. And then I went downtown on the bus and used my babysitting money to buy a pink quilted bedspread, pink ruffly curtains, and a pink fluffy furry bathmat to put on the wood floor next to my bed. I loved that room, and my poor little mother had to close the door every morning when I went to school because she couldn't believe that there was such a room in the middle of her house! But she never said a word and she always told me what a great job I had done."

Jo Packham has authored and published numerous books including Where Women Create *(Sterling, 2005). She is Editor-in-Chief of* Where Women Create *magazine and President of Chapelle, Ltd. Visit* www.wherewomencreate.com.

117

Angela Cartwright

Since the age of 16, Angela Cartwright has been passionate about photography. The mixed-media works that she creates today often integrate her photographic works as she relentlessly experiments with multi-mediums to discover new and exciting techniques that she teaches others through her workshops and many technique-based books.

INDEPENDENCE THROUGH ART

To gain inspiration, Angela Cartwright turns to one muse that is literally always at her side: her own shadow. "My shadow is a huge inspiration," says Angela. "To me, it's a symbol of who I am … where I have been and the journey I am on right now.

"I am inspired by the way my shadow dances on the ground and plays in the sun … the presence of dark and light, as well as the space between positive and negative. Following my shadow has led me deep into the discovery of myself. It's my self-portrait and I am compelled to place it in my more personal pieces of art."

Not surprisingly, capturing the essence of her shadow has involved her doing so with what she names as one of her primary creative tools: her camera. Her ability to invent ways to capture self-portrait shadows inspires not only her artistic process, but the actual art that she creates in her studio which she fondly refers to as "The Green Room."

Walking the grounds of beautiful gardens is how Angela gains inspiration. The photos she takes from such walks become transformed as she colors them and frequently incorporates them into her mixed-media works.

Angela always keeps bottles and tubes of paints and mediums close by. Even if a color is not her favorite, she loves mixing colors together to see what she can come up with.

THE GREEN ROOM

The Green Room isn't the most spacious of studios, nor the most pristine. Nevertheless, it is a space that Angela considers to be her safe haven. "I have found my work space does not need to be spacious or tidy for me to get work done. Instead, I find comfort in the unruliness of it all," says Angela.

Prior to The Green Room, Angela used to share one home office with her husband, Steve. But as her art supplies grew, they both knew that it was time for her own space. It was at about this time that Angela's daughter, Becca, was moving out of the house and into a place of her own — resulting in a perfectly timed opportunity to transform Becca's bedroom into The Green Room. Angela stores all of her fabrics, photographs, extra supplies, and paints in the room's large closet. The attached bathroom is an added convenience that allows for easy clean-up and the bathtub within the bathroom doubles as the station that stores her finished art pieces, along with work that is waiting to be shipped out.

Within easy reach in The Green Room is Angela's computer, printer, scanner, and notebooks. "I have found that having to leave to go and get something breaks my forward momentum," explains Angela. "My art space is a cocoon where I feel safe to make the art I'm meant to make."

EVOKING FEELINGS

Angela was a teenager when her passion for photography was born. At that time, the photography of Richard Avedon swept her away … influencing her to strive to take great photos. Albert Watson is another photographer who has motivated Angela to try her hand at shooting inanimate objects with passion and interest.

Once the photos are taken, Angela manipulates them with paints — causing the images to evolve into a whole new object altogether. But it doesn't stop there. She usually incorporates the altered images into larger mixed-media works where she leaves no stone unturned in terms of what she melds together. "I love textures and backgrounds made with gesso and molding pastes," says Angela. "I stamp, scrub, and sand, and am constantly experimenting with oils, acrylics, paint sticks, watercolors, and basically anything I can find to interpret my photographs in new and exciting ways."

The goal that Angela seeks with all of her work is to evoke a response — any response. She believes the piece is successful even if the response is negative. "If someone has an opinion about a piece, then it touches them somewhere. And as long as it resonates with the viewer on some level, I feel I have done what I'm supposed to do."

She remembers

Coloring pictures with crayons — often with her mom by her side — is one of Angela's fondest childhood memories. When she turned 10 years old, she traded crayons for pencils to draw large landscapes with little tiny houses and people. "And after that, my art seemed to disappear for awhile," says Angela.

"It was a few years later that photography seeped into my life and I would credit my dad with my foray into photography. He had built a darkroom in the garage and we would develop and print pictures together. It was a special time in my life."

She stays inspired

The surefire way for Angela to combat a creative rut is to take a walk with her camera … usually in her garden at home, or a museum, or in Descanso Gardens, located in Los Angeles. "I have taken thousands of photographs in Descanso Gardens. It is such a cyclical paradise and a place that really clears out my head," says Angela. "After I have walked there and stopped to smell the roses, I return home with a different perspective. I think creative ruts happen when we can't get still and centered."

SPECIAL EMERGING

Angela admits that sometimes, her best ideas don't always go according to plan in The Green Room. But making mistakes in art is something that she views as part of the creative process. "Sometimes, when you think you've just created a disaster, a lesson will be learned or a new technique will be discovered and through that process, something really special will emerge," says Angela.

Discoveries also happen for Angela in her dreams. And right now, as she is considering her desire to create sculptural pieces made of papier mâché and fabric, she describes the ideas as "just one big mess" in her head right now. "But they will eventually take form and probably appear in some dream I have … and one day, I will just start making sculptures and wonder: 'Where did this come from?' But I won't dwell on the question. I will just be grateful it's happening."

Angela Cartwright is a mixed-media artist who lives in Los Angeles, California. She is author of several books including Mixed Emulsions *(Quarry, 2007),* In This House *(Quarry, 2007), and* In This Garden *(Quarry, 2009). To learn more, visit* www.acartwrightstudio.com *or www. acartwrightstudio.blogspot.com.*

Her tips for organization & exercises to fuel creativity

TIP: Though Angela admits that her space may look disorganized, she has everything placed in a way that works for her. Her first tip is to have all supplies close at hand in individually labeled containers.

Exercise: Take a photo of your shadow with your camera. How can you position your body to evoke specific moods and feelings?

TIP: Angela uses a master notebook to keep track of all her ideas-in-progress and regularly reviews and checks things off as they get completed. "I also love Post-its® but I staple them into my master notebook so things don't get overlooked," she says.

Exercise: When collaging with photos, combat the desire for perfection by using unexpected items to attach them — like staples or masking tape, or by embedding them in gesso or paint. Observe the beauty of deliberate imperfection.

Vintage luggage pieces make great storage units for the studio. They also make great traveling studios for artists who are on the road.

GIVING BEAUTY

One of Luana's all-time favorite adages is by Confucius, who said, "Everything has beauty, but not everyone sees it." It is in fact the beauty of the world around her that inspires Luana most. "There is beauty in every person, in every living thing, in the colors and movement around us, and in the daily flow of events," she says. "I am an eternal optimist, and I try to find good in every event that occurs in my life."

The goodness, beauty, and optimism that Luana focuses on are commodities that were passed down to her by a long line of artistic ancestors. "My grandfather was quite a photographer, my great-grandmother was a California impressionist painter, and my grandmothers and great-aunts created lots of ceramics, paintings, and embroidery," she says. "There is a lot of joy and love of life that has been passed down through my family and I feel that I have an obligation to pass that joy through my art."

Luana Rubin

Luana Rubin is President of *eQuilter.com* — an online store featuring fabrics and more than 20,000 related products for quilters and sewers. Luana is also a fashion designer, painter, and quilter who frequently travels the globe to lend her expertise about color trends to leaders within the industry.

When constructing a garment or quilt, Luana believes that threads are almost as important as the fabrics. The many options that are available — including metallics and variegated — help lend the artistic polish that distinguishes a good project from a superior one.

Beauty and goodness were also gifts that Luana received from Susan Pierpont, her 7th grade art teacher who recognized early on Luana's special artistic ability. Susan gave Luana support and guidance all through high school, and also provided her with sage professional advice that helped Luana find a career path for success. "She is gone now, but her infectious enthusiasm and boundless energy are still with me," explains Luana.

Luana is inspired and creatively fueled by the reservoir of beauty and goodness that her ancestors and special mentors like Susan gave to her. And in return, Luana works hard to make sure that her own work is one that regularly gives back to people and charities in need.

Her colors
ANALOGOUS COOLS &
ONE HOT COMPLEMENTARY ACCENT

Because Luana's work involves forecasting color trends, she is drawn to fresh color combinations that are parallel to social and cultural trends. "My eye is naturally drawn to combinations of analogous cool tones with one hot complementary color like red or gold," she says.

STATE OF MIND

The "dream studio" that Luana currently enjoys is a 1200-square-foot space with continuous windows running all along the north and south walls. It is actually the second floor above the eQuilter warehouse in Boulder, Colorado, where through the windows, Luana soaks up the fabulous view of the Rocky Mountains each and every day.

The large studio comes with a walk-in closet where Luana stores her many fabrics, and a separate living room with a couch and magnificent carved opium bed from Asia. There is also a bathroom, a separate water closet with an oversized sink, and best of all: a giant 4' x 12' industrial cutting table and professional-grade dressform.

Prior to having this "dream studio," Luana spent several years working in the fashion industry as an import garment design specialist in Los Angeles, Hong Kong, and New York City. During those years, she hardly had access to the kind of square footage that she now enjoys for her creative space. "I believe that a creative space is as much a state of mind as a space to hold all your stuff," she says. Which is why even when her space was frequently only as long and wide as a singular drafting table, Luana has been able to focus and succeed.

Luana delights in selecting the fabrics that become cut into fat quarters for eQuilter's popular Fat Quarter collections.

THE COLOR OF HER ART

From childhood to her adult art career, Luana has progressed from fashion illustration and figure drawing to painting with assorted mediums — including oils, pastels, and watercolors. Eventually, Luana discovered quilting, which came very naturally and easily because of her experience as a fashion designer. "Designing and constructing a quilt is a lot easier than designing, draping, and sewing a jacket," says Luana.

"I found that very quickly I was chafing at all the rules of traditional quilting. I knew there had to be something else, and within a year had found local contemporary art quilt groups. Seeing what they were doing really gave me permission to go ahead and break all the rules … and I was very good at this. What a relief it was to find groups of like-minded people."

As Luana reflects on her very diverse creative pursuits over the years, she realizes that the foundation of her art is color. "My years of studying color through painting were very important because they taught me to see colors that most people are never aware of," she says. This penchant for color makes Luana a valuable member of the Color Marketing Group, where she is often sought out by entities, like the International Textile Expo, to offer her perspectives about color with industry leaders.

Luana Rubin is proprietor of www.eQuilter.com — *an online provider of fabrics and related products for quilters, fiber artists, and sewers. To learn more about Luana, visit* www.luanarubin.com.

Her tip for organization & exercise to fuel creativity

TIP: For those who sew, Luana recommends having not just one, but two quality sewing machines in the studio. "Having a second quality sewing machine is not a luxury, it is a necessity," she says. "A deadline is a magnet for disaster and the more urgently you work on a project, the more likely your machine will blow up or choke."

Exercise: The next time you are about to start a project, go into your yard or a nearby park and gather items that have a distinct smell — like a flower or a pinecone. Keep it nearby to use its fragrance to keep you refreshed and inspired.

Janice Lowry

Humbly, methodically, and passionately, Janice Lowry has for decades been creating assemblages, art journals, artwear, collages, and art zines. Her works cleverly juxtapose the events and news of our world alongside her unique and personal perspective to magically produce experiences that transform the viewer.

OUTWARD & INWARD

Aside from the daily ruts that many artists encounter, sometimes Janice Lowry has been known to battle creative blocks that last several months. Recently when Janice was experiencing this type of long-term creative block, she was able to regain inspiration once again by looking at a piece of Mexican folk art. "It was an 'aha' moment," says Janice. "I had had the Mexican folk art piece for more than 40 years and in this moment, it is what got me going. I started working. Not making exact copies but being so very inspired by the colors and vibrancy of this art."

Looking outward toward elements that can ignite passion — like Mexican folk art, nature, books, and people — are what help Janice get back in the groove.

Aside from the lengthier ruts that require a jolt of outward stimulation, Janice looks inward on a day-to-day basis to find the inspiration that she needs. And this daily inspiration is found through the process of writing. "When I feel uninspired, I know I need to start writing my morning pages and get into the process of listening … largely to my inner voice" says Janice.

Though her assemblages often start from a stream of consciousness process, they usually conclude as pieces that symbolize major moments in Janice's life, or significant events from the world around her.

FROM LIMITED TO UNLIMITED

Janice has always made certain to have a space to make art. "As a teenager living at home with white shag carpet, my paintings were stored under my bed," recalls Janice. "My next space as a young married mother was an 'art closet.' All my supplies and projects were stored next to the washer and dryer."

During those years when space was limited, Janice would take out whatever current project she was working on and focus her efforts on the kitchen counter. "I was then able to orchestrate the lives of my young children," she says. "This was the last time that my art space was so limited. Since then, I have always had a designated room to make art."

Currently, the space that Janice calls her studio is actually a loft that is designed for the purpose of making art. The floors are made out of cement with 14-feet ceilings. There are windows on three sides of the space. "My studio overlooks a courtyard so I also have a bit of nature looking through my windows." And housed on the walls of her studio are the assemblages that Janice is famous for.

Her tip for organization & exercise to fuel creativity

TIP: In order to keep her mountains of supplies needed to create collages and assemblages, Janice places everything in plastic containers and labels the fronts of the containers.

Exercise: Close your eyes and place your finger onto the page of a magazine or newspaper. Open your eyes and wherever your finger has landed, start writing or doodling something in response to what your finger points to.

THE ART OF REPORTAGE

Since the age of 11, Janice has been writing and keeping journals. To date, she has completed nearly 130 journals that chronicle her life and the life that has happened around her while growing up. When she was a little girl, she used to call these journals her diaries. More recently, she has started calling them "reportages" — which reflects the essence of what she feels she is doing. "Through these books, I am reporting what is happening around me ... of course through the unique lens of how I see things, based on who I am and what I have experienced," says Janice.

This collection of journals is impressive to anyone who has a chance to see it. And very soon, the nearly 130 art journals will be available for anyone who wants to view them as they have been accepted by the Smithsonian Archives of American Art to become part of their permanent collection.

Aside from the journals, Janice also creates assemblages, collages, paintings, and assorted creations involving sewing and needlework. "It seems there is this art wheel that I have been on for over 30 years and I like it very much," says Janice.

Her colors

WARM & MUTED SHADES • BLACK • TURQUOISE

Warm and muted shades are what Janice is drawn to. "The warm shades are usually mixed with a bit of black," she says. "The colors then become somber. From there, I like to place a pure and unexpected color like turquoise ... which creates a contrast, causing one color to appear darker and the other one more vibrant."

EXPLORING NEXT

So what's next for Janice? "Funny you should ask," she says. "I plan on taking an encaustic painting class … I just want to learn how to use this medium and see where this might lead."

The luxury that Janice is finally able to enjoy where she can explore new mediums like encaustic wax isn't something she takes for granted. When she was a single mom with children and no career, she applied to the Art Center and in less than four years, she earned a BFA and an MFA. "Being single and an artist is a tough path," explains Janice. "But the group of teachers at Art Center College of Design taught me to love my work and to trust my process."

With the many, many people who follow and collect the work of Janice, it would be hard to name who might be her biggest fan. But chances are that within the top five of her fans would include her husband, Jon. "He taught me to love and trust myself and the world I live in," says Janice.

Janice Lowry is a mixed-media artist who lives in southern California. She is an editorial advisor for Somerset Studio *magazine. To learn more about her art, visit* www.janicelowry.com.

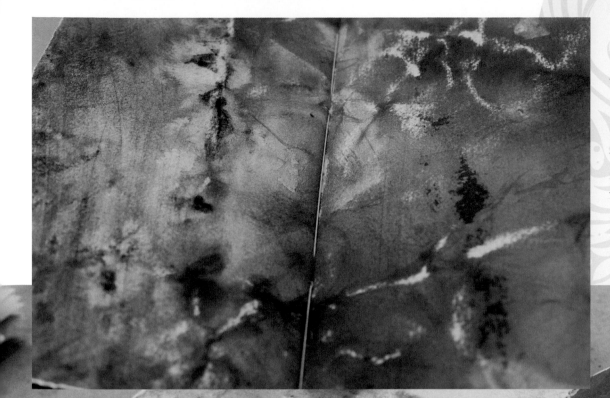

Janice likes to fill her art journal pages by loading them with layers of color. Once the color is done, she comes back to them when the time is right to add words and other artistic enhancements.

Line Christensen

Line Christensen understands logic and science but when really tough decisions need to be made, she looks to the sound of her heart. By doing so, she has learned huge lessons about business and inspiration and quality living through many interesting jobs over the past several years — including jobs with IKEA®, Converse®, Bodyglove, and Anthropologie. Line applies the best of what she has learned into her cooking school (Line's Open Kitchen) and unique line of art clothing for children (Mrs. Piggy's Trend).

BREATHING IN TEMPO

Taking walks and focusing on all that is involved with the act of walking … breathing in, breathing out, putting one step in front of the other, and then the other, and then the other … this is what inspires and fuels Line Christensen. "I am a girl who gets my inspiration just by taking a walk … my walks have been very important for me," she says. "I try to do it two to three times a week where I pick out a place that I want to explore. It could be a beach, a special street, or a familiar road in the city. I explore the people, the food, the nature."

Aside from the walks, Line also turns to music to gain inspiration and energy during her creative process. "When I'm sewing, I like to listen to jazz or classical music but when I'm feeling wild, Bruce Springsteen is my favorite," she says. "He is one of my heroes … he grew up being told he could not read or write and that he would amount to nothing. He worked hard and believed in himself and made it happen. Bruce's story is what I point to when I tell my children that as long as you can breathe in, you can breathe out too, but in your unique and individual tempo."

INTERNATIONAL HEART

Prior to her current home in the United States, Line lived in Germany, Spain, and England. "I am a Danish girl who was brought up in a home full of academics. I was trained to make decisions based on logic and scientific reasoning," she says. "But things can't always be resolved by scientific reasoning … frequently, I have to listen to my heart, which always seems to speak louder than my head. And I think that is why I am here today."

Since she was a little girl, Line dreamed of owning a store. And by following her heart, she was eventually able to earn a bachelor's degree in textile design, leading to her first job at a Swedish clothing company. Eventually, she would move on to work for Converse and then to Bodyglove.

At the age of 27, Line had her first child and transitioned into one of her all-time favorite jobs of working for IKEA, where she was instrumental in building its successful brand. While she was raising a family and working for IKEA, Line also worked for a time designing and selling furniture to shops in Europe. "It was a scary experience because some of the big companies ordered more than I could produce," she says. "I was working very hard with the furniture business but also juggling my family and my job at IKEA. I don't know what I was thinking but I was learning a lot."

By keeping yarns of all colors stored in a basket together rather than sorting them by color, Line frequently stumbles upon color combinations that she might not otherwise think of.

She stays
inspired

In order to stay
inspired, Line puts
more responsibility
onto her plate. "I've
always found that it
is when I'm busiest
that I am the most
creative," she says.

FROM THE KITCHEN TO MRS. PIGGY

When Line and her family moved to the United States, she decided to pursue another one of her passions — cooking. "I went to Sur La Table near where we lived and did some cooking classes for them," she says. Before I knew it, I was behind the counter teaching cooking. Some of my friends told me to do it from home so I did, and my cooking school was born (Line's Open Kitchen)."

In between her cooking, Line still wanted to do more and landed a job working for the creative team at Anthropologie. Soon after, Line launched her children's clothing line called Mrs. Piggy's Trend (*www.mrspiggystrend.com*). As a mother to four children, Line's designs are inspired to create what she calls "wearable clothes for imaginative play." "The clothes I make have to be a joy to wear so that children can jump and run around and still look like kings and queens," she explains.

The common denominator for both the food she cooks and the clothes she makes is that she creates with organic materials. Says Line: "In my opinion, whether it's food or clothes, it's not quantity but quality that will make you happy and healthy."

Her colors
ALL PALETTES

Because Line works in so many different color palettes and sees the strength and beauty of each palette, she is unable to claim a favorite.

"I do not have a favorite color palette," she says. "I love each color palette in its own way and work around them to get the best results for what I am working on."

FROM DESIGN TO FULFILLMENT

To make all of this happen, Line uses all parts of her house — her kitchen, her living room, and almost all other areas of her home to design clothes, cook food, take online orders, and manage the assembly and fulfillment process. It isn't quite the store that Line imagined as a child … it's actually a larger hub that encompasses creativity for the body and soul.

Line Christensen lives in southern California. To learn more about her line of children's clothing, visit her Web site at www.mrspiggystrend.com.

Her organizational tip & exercise to fuel creativity

TIP: More than ever before, Line recognizes the need to be a good steward and try to upcycle discards whenever possible. "I always recycle glass jars and I use them to store bits and bobs for my sewing and crafting projects," she says.

Exercise: The next time you're about to throw out everyday containers such as cereal boxes, jam jars, egg cartons, and other "discards," try to embellish them into a functional storage unit for the studio.

A simple length of jute string with mini clothespins are what Line uses to store small treasures that serve as fresh and playful inspiration.

Jenny Doh

....

Jenny Doh is Editor-in-Chief & Director of Publishing for *Somerset Studio* and its sister publications. Through her leadership, Stampington & Company has experienced tremendous growth, where she leads the recruitment and production of more than 30 titles per year. In recognition of her role in publishing, Jenny was selected as part of the Folio: 40 — an annual list of 40 influencers and innovators within the magazine industry, as identified by *Folio* magazine.

ORANGE JUICE & BANANA

The written word is what inspires Jenny. Whether it's a single word or a sentence or an article or a book, Jenny has found that words can have a huge impact on the way humans think, feel, and behave.

At the age of 7, Jenny and her family left their home in Seoul, Korea, and moved to the United States to make their way in a land where opportunity grew on trees for those who were willing to work hard. "There were only four words I knew in English at that time: 'yes,' 'no,' 'orange juice,' and 'banana.' I remember thinking on the airplane that even though I wouldn't be able to converse with Americans because I only knew four words, I would at least be able to read books," she says. "And then panic hit me when I realized that all the books would be written in English!"

As soon as she entered elementary school in Bakersfield, California, Jenny excelled with the written word. "I'm not sure why it was so easy for me but I remember being able to read and write words and sentences that my peers struggled with. I knew at an early age that the written word was my friend."

Today, as she oversees the art and words that go into *Somerset Studio* and its sister publications, Jenny is at the height of her creativity when editing or writing content. When she is in her home studio, words remain her main source of inspiration for the art that she creates. "When I'm making a rubber-stamped card or other mixed-media work, words have a way of beautifully permeating all that I make," she says.

No matter where she goes, Jenny always has her organizer close by — a binder system by FranklinCovey® that she has used for more than two decades. She loves to embellish her binders that she replaces every couple of years.

You are
who you
choose to be

AFTER THE HOMEWORK

After a full day's work, Jenny is usually juggling typical mommy duties of cooking dinner and overseeing her children's homework. "I love my family but I actually sort of dread the whole homework thing. It's really quite stressful. But that's OK. Helping with homework and doing the dishes and doing the laundry are things that help me stay grounded and focused on what's really important," she says. "And the great thing about household chores is that once they're done, I can retire into my very own special place to continue with my creative pursuits."

"The great thing about my studio is that it's equipped with an iMac computer that is set up so I am connected with the servers at the office and can oversee the production of our publications at any time. Aside from that, the iMac lets me continue to scout for content as I browse through blogs and Web sites. And of course I also use my iMac to manage my own blog, which I have come to cherish as a very important creative outlet."

Jenny's studio used to be the formal dining room, which she and her husband converted into her studio. "I used to actually have all my stuff crammed into a small closet, but eventually, we realized that I needed more space. And given that my career is all about arts and crafts, it made great sense to be able to have a space where I could work on my career by working on my arts and crafts."

To make the most of the natural light that flows into her studio, Jenny fills vintage jars with her collection of buttons and baubles and lines them up next to the window.

Her colors

RED • WHITE • BLACK

Jenny's favorite color is red. "It's a color that exudes strength, confidence, and power," she says. "And when you combine the strength of red with the serenity and elegance of white and black, a wonderful balance is achieved."

KNITTING IN MY SLEEP

Many within the art and crafting community would consider the magazines that Jenny makes as art. But aside from the publications, Jenny is an avid knitter, quilter, cellist, photographer, and creator of assorted mixed-media projects. "I've been knitting since I was 6 years old," she says. "And more than any other medium, yarn and needles make up what I consider to be my forté. If I had to, I think I could knit in my sleep."

Aside from knitting, Jenny's assorted projects frequently turn up within the pages of various Stampington & Company publications. These projects usually involve rubber stamps and paper, including her regular feature in *Take Ten* magazine, where she writes a column titled "The Art of Minimalism." "The idea for this column is to show readers that beautiful art doesn't always have to involve layers and layers of stuff," she says. "For me, it is when artistic restraint can be exercised with thoughtful juxtaposition of elements that true beauty and artistic depth emerge. 'Artistic minimalism' is different from 'simple' or 'trite' or 'casual.' It's about deliberate balance and very careful placement that can yield quite elegant, extraordinary results. It's actually not so easy to execute."

For more than a year, Jenny has also become a passionate photographer. "I have a Canon 30D, which is an amazing camera," she says. "When I decided to start a blog, I realized that I wanted to post beautiful photos, which led me to research and invest in the Canon. Aside from the photos I take for my blog, some of my shots also make their way into my magazines. There's a lot more I need to learn but with the little knowledge that I have, I'm able to take some pretty wonderful photos. I love it."

She stays inspired

When Jenny encounters a creative rut, she turns to music. "I play the cello but I also sing and play the guitar and the piano," she says. "And when I am stuck with something that I'm writing or making, I turn to one of my instruments and after a tune or two, I'm recharged and ready to get back to work.

A papier mâché dressform is where Jenny stores art jewelry that she has either received as gifts or created on her own — a quick and easy way to keep things visible and untangled.

Her tip for organization & exercise to fuel creativity

TIP: Jenny's greatest advice for organization is to set deadlines and aim to beat them. "Even if a project doesn't have a real deadline, I think it's important to create a self-imposed one," she says. "When there really is an actual deadline, I psych myself out to pace myself so I can beat the real deadline by a day. This way, if an emergency ever comes up, I may end up not being able to beat a deadline, but I'll always meet it."

Exercise: Get a stack of shipping tags and a rubber stamp and stamp the image onto the tags. Once you have a stack of stamped tags, go back and color each one using different mediums like paint, colored pencils, and markers, to achieve different effects.

DOING ART

For Jenny, art is about doing. "It's not about envying, wishing, grumbling, griping, complaining, criticizing, regretting, bemoaning, or any of the many blocks that become erected by negativity and passivity," she says.

"When I hear someone say 'Oh I wish I could knit,' I say, 'You don't need to wish. Just do it. It's not that hard. Go get some yarn and needles, find a knitting friend, or get a book, or go online, and for goodness sake, knit!' Same goes for everything else. I don't like excuses that waste time pointing to blocks or walls that get in the way of life. We all have access to the same hours in a day. I choose to use those hours to make a life that I love."

Jenny Doh is Editor-in-Chief & Director of Publishing for Stampington & Company. To learn about the magazines she oversees, visit www. stampington.com. *To learn about her art and life, visit her blog at* www. jennydoh.typepad.com.

She remembers

Ever since she can remember, Jenny was knitting. "My grandmother is the one who taught me to knit when I was a little girl. She was an amazing knitter and creative genius," says Jenny. "Not only could she knit, she could sew almost anything. I remember times when I'd point to skirts and dresses in a store or a catalog that I liked and before I knew it, she would have those items all sewn up for me to wear. It was magic."

Today, Jenny is an avid knitter and crocheter and frequently finds herself channeling the spirit of her grandmother when she embarks on any creative project.

Credits

PHOTOGRAPHERS

Alisa Burke: pages 102, 105

Angela Cartwright: pages 118–119, 122

Jenny Doh: pages 105, 128, 130, 133

Joanna Figueroa: page 98

Michael Garland: pages 18–23, 48–53, 62–65, 68, 80–85, 98–101, 103–104, 106–111, 120–123, 129–132, 134–137

Pam Garrison: pages 62, 64–67

Steve Guillion: page 118

Amy Hanna: pages 48–52

Ryne Hazen: pages 30–35

Paula Jansen: pages 92–97

Johanna Love: pages 138–143

Steve Mann: pages 86–91

Saul Martinez: pages 10–17

Emilie Matthiesen: page 24

Hanne Matthiesen: pages 24–29

Laurie Mika: pages 70–71

Colin Mika: page 68

Shane O'Neil: pages 54–61

Anna Paschall: pages 30, 32, 33, 35

Cory Ryan: pages 42–47

Melissa Sands: pages 36–41

Susan Tuttle: pages 72–79

Dana Waldon: pages 124–127

Zac Williams: pages 112–117

Index